Voices from the
Bottom of the Bowl

ABOUT THE AUTHOR

Born in 1956, Akira Arai is a film writer and producer of note credited for international projects as head of his own studio, Kinetique. *A Caring Man*, which he submitted to the Golden Elephant Award enticed by its global vision, marks his debut as a novelist. He lives in Tokyo, Japan.

Voices from the
Bottom of the Bowl

A Folk History of
Teton Valley, Idaho, 1823–1952

THOMAS EDWARD CHENEY

University of Utah Press
Salt Lake City

∞ The paper in this book meets the standards for permanence and durability established by the Committee on Production Guidelines for Book Longevity of the Council on Library Resources

Library of Congress Cataloging-in-Publication Data

Cheney, Thomas Edward, 1901–
    Voices from the bottom of the bowl : a folk history of Teton Valley, Idaho, 1823–1952 / Thomas Edward Cheney.
        p.   cm.
    ISBN 0-87480-368-3
    1. Teton River Valley (Idaho)—Social life and customs. 2. Teton River Valley (Idaho)—Biography. 3. Cheney, Thomas Edward, 1901——Childhood and youth. I. Title.
    F752.T5C47 1991
    978.7'55—dc20   91–50330
                                                                         CIP

To Renee and Karla Dawn, best of daughters,
who may see herein something of their heritage

Contents

Acknowledgments

S ince most of the stories herein were contributed to me during the first half of the twentieth century and not recorded at the time, they are oral folk history. I am indebted to the relatives, friends, and associates who gave me the drama and delight they provide. Each story is true in its core. The recorder of such stories must provide creative detail which may or may not be accurate. If I have misrepresented anything I apologize. I have changed some names in order not to let any skeletons out of closets.

Dr. John B. Harris, a trained judge of literature, read my manuscript and appraised every item in it. His suggestions led me to prepare the work for publication.

Introduction

My valley is situated in the front of the seat of the chair that is the state of Idaho, a valley surrounded by mountains, on the eastern side of which is the Teton Range separating Idaho from Wyoming. From the southeastern end of the Teton Range rises Trail Creek, which joins with other creeks in its twenty-mile course to become the Teton River. This valley, this earthen bowl that catches the water from the snows of the mountains, is a broken dish with a crack through which the Teton River reaches the mighty Snake. On the bottom of the bowl, where Trail Creek comes out of the mountains, is the town of Victor, established on its banks.

Like a culture in a bowl I am a form of life generated there. In this book are items stored by the computer programmer of life somewhere in the recesses of my grey matter. They were fed into the storage cells sometime since I was born (the year Queen Victoria died) and the present. They are accurate as memory is accurate, biased as mortals may be biased, and romanticized as time and imagination unconsciously romanticize.

The book is autobiographical, set chiefly in the first quarter of the twentieth century, the developmental years of my life in the valley. My people were in the vanguard of adventurous frontiersmen who first pastured their flocks in this Rocky Mountain high country. In this account I am Thomas Hardy's Clym Yarbright in my Egdon Heath. This autobiography presents the history of a town, folk history that focuses on the individual rather than on the group. In this sense it is an Ernie Pyle type of reporting. The setting, Teton Valley, is itself an entity, somewhat of an actor in the drama, as the Mississippi River is an entity in *The Adventures of Huckleberry Finn*.

Ours was a uniquely American heritage. We were children of hinterland customs and hinterland theology. Though the dominant faith of the people was Mormon, the heterogeneous mass—Mormons, Jack Mormons, Protestants, and unchurched people—gave primary attention to realities around them and to earthly survival rather than to heavenly hopes. Among pioneers a basic support and love for each other prevailed.

The people of my valley are in me and I in them, for I saw the same sights, smelled the same smells, heard the same sounds, felt the same winds, tasted the same foods as they. Isolated and insular, we shared experiences and knowledge. We suffered with the same communicable diseases, used the same medications, cried over the same sorrows, and laughed at the same jokes. Herein lie universals.

The book contains sixty-five items of history, short stories, and vignettes featuring over fifty major characters acting or being acted upon, showing experiences, frustrations, and ideals as they interact with each other and with me. Some stories are interrelated. Some characters appear again and again in different segments. The matriarch of the book, my mother, appears in twenty-four stories, one of them near the beginning and another at the end. She is the binding twine holding the whole together.

The characters—my mother, stepfathers, siblings, teachers, peers, and community leaders molded my thought and guided my action. The murderer, adulterers, bank robber, saloonkeeper, bootlegger, the profane, the selfish, the lazy also taught me.

Some of these stories have been recorded since 1945 and, after slight exposure, have lain in my cabinet. I offer them now partly because family, friends, and associates urge me not to let them die. If the reader finds chaff among the wheat, not spotted by my failing vision, he has no obligation to devour it.

Hunters and Homesteaders, 1823–1901

PIERRE'S HOLE

I n the days of youth and daydreams I often climbed up the mountain above our farm. I walked through the trees on pine grass and out onto the steep ridge and grassy slope to the old cedar tree, standing alone, braving wind and weather and providing shade for weary hikers. Sitting under its gnarled branches, I could see the valley, my valley, below, about a dozen miles wide and twice as long, lying like an oblong gravy bowl in the mountains. Looking north from my vantage point, about twelve miles away I could see the mighty and rugged peaks called the Tetons, an Indian name, a word for teats, as if Mother Nature were lying on her back getting a suntan. The mountain range stretched on north toward Yellowstone Park, some fifty miles away from my station. The mountains tapered off to the northwest into rolling hills through which the Teton River passed to find its way to the Snake. To the west the mountains on my left reached higher to catch the first rays of the rising sun. Behind me to the south rose steep and lofty cliffs curving toward the east. There I could see little glimpses of the road winding up, back and forth through tree-covered slopes to a formidable pass leading to Jackson's Hole, Wyoming. Crossing that road I could see a ravine, a steep slope, where an avalanche had swept trees away and left a rocky crevice, a memorial to me of a man I knew who was buried, crushed, and smothered there in a mass of sliding snow.

It was easy to follow the route of Trail Creek from the point where it emerged from the forest at the foot of the mountain by the Jackson road. Cottonwood trees found rooting along its meandering route and marked its way through the valley to the Teton River. Smaller creeks—Warm Creek straight below me, Fox Creek, Smith, Pine, Bitch, and Teton—all snaked their way to the river marked by trees and willows.

This valley was my Idaho, gem of the mountains, where to see sunrise or sunset on the endless mountain range was an unparalleled experience.

These mountains, part of the watershed of the mighty thousand-mile-long Snake River, dramatize the eternality of the circle of water from sea to air, to wind, cloud, rain or snow, creek, river, and back to the sea.

Coming down from the mountain, I could see the valley lying before me like a crazy quilt with seams of green thread holding together big blocks of grey and purple sage, smaller blocks of dark alfalfa green, light wheat green, and miniature blocks of nature's mix.

Long ago fur traders and mountain men had found Shoshone Indians living along Idaho's roaring river, Indians with whom communication consisted strongly of snakelike gestures. These Indians also had carved ugly snake heads of wood and placed them along trails, possibly to spook strangers. Naturally white men called these Indians Snakes and the river the Snake.

In the first half of the nineteenth century the upper Snake River country became a favorite stomping ground for British and American fur traders and trappers. Beaver-rich Teton Valley, Idaho, got its original name, Pierre's Hole, from Pierre Tevanilagen, an Iroquois Indian fur trader for the Hudson's Bay Company. In those first lucrative fur-trading days between 1822 and 1840, Pierre found the valley and trapped in it. Colonel William Henry Ashley, with whom Pierre worked, sold 9,700 pounds of pelts in 1825 for $48,000 and a $60,000 lot the next year.

Among fur traders William Sublette was prominent in Pierre's Hole. In 1829 he conducted a rendezvous in Wind River, Wyoming, an area about forty miles northeast of Pierre's Hole, after which in August he went by appointment to meet Jackson in the beautiful Wyoming valley that bears his name. Another partner, the valiant and hardy mountain man Jedediah Smith, planned to meet them there. Sublette and Jackson waited for their senior partner to arrive. When he did not appear, they searched for and found him with four other men trapping in Pierre's Hole, where they combined forces and trapped the remainder of the summer. That year Sublette and Jackson went east with 190 packs of furs worth $80,000.

Three years later Sublette, with others, conducted the most notable event occurring in Teton Valley, Idaho, in fur-trading years, the Rendezvous of 1832. The obvious purpose of these gatherings was trade of supplies and furs. Indians, working for traders, as well as white men, working for the Rocky Mountain Fur Company and the American Fur Company, brought pelts and supplies for barter.

The Pierre's Hole Rendezvous became a social event of great amplitude. The mixture of about five hundred white men and five hundred Indians ate, drank raw alcohol, which released inhibitions, and in general raised hell.

They raced horses and gambled. Some lost their year's earnings. Others grappled with squaws in love and lust. Near the closing time of the celebration, warriors of the Blackfoot tribe of Indians attacked the gathering with intent to plunder. Sublette, then thirty-five years of age, organized the defense. The vicious fight continued until thirty-five Blackfoot Indians were killed and many wounded, and the battle was won by the traders. Of their group, five mountain men and seven Flathead and Nez Perce Indians were killed.

Little of note has been recorded of Teton Valley following the Rendezvous of 1832 and the inception of permanent settlers more than a half century later. By that time the name "Pierre's Hole" had been abandoned.

In my school days earth's own story of history spoke to me of the Indian-trapper days. I found on our farm adjoining the town of Victor two arrowheads carefully shaped, both almost transparent flint, one pale blue in color and about two inches long, the other red-brown in color and longer and bigger.

Don Carlos Driggs, Homesteader

The Homestead Act of Congress of 1862 allowed aspiring landowners to push into unsettled areas of the country to secure for themselves 160 acres of land practically free. The first permanent settlers of my valley were sturdy pioneers of courage and vision. One of these was Don Carlos Driggs.

In the center of Teton Valley is the town of Driggs, with a population at present of one thousand. It has the distinction of being the first permanent settlement in the valley. The historian Howard R. Driggs says that in 1893 it boasted enough settlers to petition the U.S. government for a post office, and that when officials in Washington, D.C., received the petition they found so many "Driggs" signatures that they could logically call the post office "Driggs."

In truth the town was settled by four Driggs brothers—Benjamin, Don Carlos, Parley, and Leland. It was Don who first entered Pierre's Hole, and in 1888 he staked his homestead claim of 160 acres of Idaho land. On his homestead he built the first log cabin in the valley.

Don C. Driggs became the leading citizen of the valley deservedly. When critics said, "Weather here is nine months winter and three months late in the fall," he cited the beauty of the mountains, the cleanness of the water, the freshness of the air, the odor of clover, accessible forests, plentiful game and fish. He built and operated the first store in the valley. His customers, he said, were Mormon settlers, trappers, prospectors, and outlaws.

Don C. Driggs was appointed the first postmaster of Driggs by President Grover Cleveland in December 1894. Ten years later, in 1904, the town was officially incorporated with Don C. Driggs as the first mayor. By 1914 he was a state legislator, county commissioner, and Latter-day Saint stake president. It was that year that the Union Pacific Railroad completed its line to Driggs and beyond to its terminus at Victor.

In August, 1913, a celebration commemorated completion of the railroad, the biggest celebration held in the valley since Indians and trappers met in the Pierre's Hole Rendezvous. That day the big steam locomotive pulled the first passenger-freight train into the valley and opened the celebration with its powerful whistle blasting the air and reverberating from the mountains in dying echoes. A mass of people, the largest crowd I had ever seen, filled the town. A spike had been left undriven at a point by the new railroad station. The locomotive with its trailing cars had puffed its way to within twenty feet of the spot and stood there breathing softly as the ceremony took place and Don C. Driggs swung the eight-pound hammer to drive the final spike into the tie to hold the rail firmly in place.

THOMAS AND ELIZA CHENEY

Before I spoke with the voice of a man, I read a biographical book, *Uncle Nick Among the Shoshones*. It was the story of Nicholas Wilson, a boy kidnapped from the whites and reared by Indians. The story aroused my deep emotions, gave me vicarious adventures, and provided me a hero to worship, a hero more personably potent no doubt because Nick Wilson was a brother of my Aunt Alice.

The Wilsons ventured into outlying Indian country. There Indians stole their son, and a squaw made the handsome boy her own. Uncle Selar Cheney joined the Wilsons in their adventures and married their daughter Alice.

When the Driggs men were building log homes and clearing land in the center of Teton Valley, Selar Cheney and the enterprising Wilsons drove their cattle on through the valley and up and over the treacherous pass to establish ranches in Jackson Hole.

If Selar Cheney had any cross to bear in his activities, he bore it without physical scars or serious privations. He raised his eyes to the stone majesty of the Teton Mountains fit for deer and eagles. He saw the luscious green of the big earth and the star-studded blue of the sky. He heard the breeze in the trees, the songs of birds in various voices, and the distant staccato bark of coyotes. He smelled the aroma of grass and flowers—and in all felt free. His expressions of love for the upper Snake River country reached relatives in Utah. Shortly, by his colorful invitations, by government reports of homestead opportunities, and by Mormon spirit of empire, a half dozen young families, all relatives of Selar and the Wilsons, migrated to Teton Valley in the last ten years of the nineteenth century. Among these were my parents, Thomas and Eliza Cheney.

Pioneering in that cold country proved to be more strenuous for Thomas and Eliza than for Selar and the Wilsons, who had already learned the Indian secrets of survival—how to satisfy hunger with elk, deer, and fish meat, with berries and roots. They knew how to use nature's raw materials for shelter and clothing, and how to communicate and deal with Indians. Though Thomas and Eliza were not well schooled in those arts, they knew pioneering with its accompanying work, work, work and save, save, save.

From Mother I heard but little about privations, misfortunes, and disaster; yet little slivers of sad memories often emerged such as losing sheep— ewes, almost ready to lamb, killed by coyotes, robbing them of future security—an empty flour bin, using strips of elk hide instead of hinges on the outside door, letting the door drag and hang loosely while they waited for buying power to get hardware. Her longer accounts lengthened the joys and shortened the sorrows, as did the following:

"The meadows smelled of clover, the mountains of pine needles, and Trail Creek rolled and rushed a powerful stream in the spring when we arrived in the valley in 1893. I was young then, eager for life and adventure. This was better than the unfertile, alkaline soil of Emery County, Utah, this basin with mountainsides soft with soil, better for me and my husband to tame, better air for our little girl to breathe.

"That year winter threatened before we had hinges on the door of the cabin and before Thomas had gathered enough wild hay to feed the animals through the winter. But to work for survival takes no prodding. We met the challenge. The warmth of the fireplace and all such little joys hypnotically obliterated inconveniences.

"The dozen families homesteading land along Trail Creek helped each other. If we ran out of .38 shells to kill a deer or an elk, we could trade something for them; if we needed sulphur matches or a start of yeast, we could borrow; if we got sick, we had help. This small community with a common cause built a comradeship of empathy for each other.

"Our colonizing went well. Eight years later we had established a farm, our dairy herd had grown, our sheep multiplied, and we had more of the necessities of life in supply. It was August 1901. We had three girls now—Areatha, 9, Cora, 7, and Naomi, 2, and we expected another child in November.

"Thomas and I were about to reach the first base in the home run of life when tragedy overtook us. Thomas had been miserable with toothache from a badly decayed molar. To ease the pain until he could go out of the valley to get the tooth extracted, he had taken laudanum. One noontime he came to the house with swollen jaw and fevered brow. The fever would not yield to any medications we knew, nor to faithful or fervent prayers. Thomas died of blood poison four days later."

ANOTHER MOUTH TO FEED

From the midwife, Lizzy Curtis, who delivered me to my mother at a cost of $3.00, came an interesting folk belief:

Eliza sits with needle and cloth
As summer days pass by
Sewing for her unborn child,
For her apron now hangs high.

"You are home early, Thomas dear;
Why do you come so soon?"
"I'm sick, dear wife, I'm sick enough
To rest this afternoon."

Oh, he grew sick and very sick—
"Give me cold water, Dear,
My mouth is dry. I'm burning hot.
My life, my life I fear.

"I feel the death grip in my throat,
The mist dark in my eye—
Greet my unborn child for me,
And bid the girls good-bye."

Many days did Eliza walk
Up and down the floor
With salt tears falling from her eyes,
For him she'd see no more.

The ice grew thick, the cold wind blew,
Eliza worked with care
For food and clothes and firewood
For three small girls so fair.

Then one night Eliza spoke,
"Call help, for time is nigh."
And she gripped her hands in agony
As pain blinded her eye.

The midwife worked with skillful hands,
Did well the birthing deed.
"Eliza, dear, you have a boy,
Another mouth to feed.

"Your son will be a special man,
For he came wrapped in the veil,
And all on whom this favor falls
Will live to much avail.

"He'll be a master of the land
Or a merchant of the sea.
Riches and honor he will gain
And be free from the hanging tree."

I never heard of this special design to be gifted that fate had placed on me until after Mother's death in 1952. In an old trunk in a storeroom my sisters found a large envelope containing folded butcher's paper on which was attached a dried-up membrane. The fact that Mother had never told me about my fate suggests that she never had believed in the prediction or that she lost faith in it as I developed.

The folklore of the veil or caul was widespread. This caul is part of the amnion, the inner membrane of the sac enveloping the fetus in the uterus. The folklorist Wayland Hand found the belief in variations in Alabama, Louisiana, Illinois, and Nova Scotia. Some folk simply said that the veiled person would have special insights. Most, however, attached the insights to the unknown world of the spiritual. It was believed that people who had died are walking all around us, but only those born with the caul can see and communicate with them and gain from them some kinds of divine insights.

I want to witness here that I have never seen a ghost except for those pseudo ones of Disneyland and Halloween; I have none of the insights of a Hamlet, nor has any ghost talked to me either to advise me to seek revenge, to direct my life, or to give me a gift of faith. I am glad, however, that some-one removed the veil covering my face when I was born so that I could breathe.

Stepfather Peter S. Durney, 1904–1910

THE COFFIN MAKER AND THE MYSTERY OF DEATH

Before my third birthday my mother married again. Her second husband was a widower, Peter S. Durney, a vigorous man of about forty, an ambitious, enterprising farmer and carpenter. He owned a farm that lay at the mouth of Pole Canyon on the south end of the valley above the big String Canal. On the farm, about fifty yards above the tall brick house at the foot of the mountain, a warm spring bubbled up forming Warm Creek, which ran by the house free of ice and snow in winter and lined with watercress in spring. It provided culinary water for the home, drinking water for livestock, irrigation water for the farm, and finally contributed its mite to the Teton River.

The farmhouse stood among tall trees in a setting of beauty and peace. The pine-scented air, the melody of the mountain stream, the songs of birds in the trees, the sounds like aeolian harps of breezes in the branches, joined together to touch the heart. Behind the house and attached to it by a boardwalk porch was Pa's carpenter shop with its long workbench, like the bed of a wagon with a vise on the end where he clamped boards to hold them tight. On the wall hung saws, braces, bits, hammers, and the like. On shelves were other tools not hung on the wall or kept in the chest below.

Pa made coffins for anyone who died in the valley. He had to work fast, for dead bodies could not be kept long in summer. I remember how lovely these coffins were, all lined inside with pink or white satin quilting and beautified with chrome hinges, handles, and locks.

I must have been five or six years old at the time. I had never related these pretty boxes Pa made with death before this night. I only knew that Pa's magic, working with nice-smelling boards and screws and paint and glue and cloth, could create pretty boxes.

Mama felt sorry for Pa, who had to work all night to make a coffin for Liza Griffith.

I liked the shop, especially when Pa was sawing and planing boards, the shavings coming off in little curls, leaving the smell of the pitch-filled wood in the air. It was dark when I went out to watch Pa, the pine trees looking dark in the moonlight and aspen leaves trembling in shadows, but the carpenter shop shone light and warm in the white glow of Pa's gaslight with the mantle dazzling the eyes like the sun. I went to the far corner, where Pa told me to go and where I stayed faithfully, for Pa got angry and scolded me if I got in his way. It was then that a knock came at the door and a huge man smoking a cigarette and wearing a big black mustache came into the shop. It was Henry Griffith.

"Pete," the man said in a loud, gruff voice, "I want you to make the coffin big enough for the baby too."

"Is it dead?" Pa asked.

"No, it ain't dead, Pete, but it can't live without a mother."

Pa turned to me and said, "Thomas, it is your bedtime. Go."

I looked with fear at the big man with the black mustache, yet I had to go by him to get out the door. He moved aside. I kept an eye on him as I passed so I could dodge if he hit at me. I hated him.

In the house my mother sat in the rocker nursing my baby sister. What if the baby were buried alive in a coffin? I went to bed. All I could see was a little baby alive under the ground in a coffin. The horror! The horror of a vision of a child buried alive. I covered my head, trying to escape.

In the days that followed, my mother assured me that the big man's baby would not be buried alive; yet the terror of that view of death that came to me persisted even after the dead mother was buried and the baby, still alive, lived on. Day after day my mind continued to brood on the mystery of death, the totally unfathomable finality of a living person becoming lifeless and being buried in the ground.

PROVOKED TO ANGER

A child of eight, I lacked the physical rough-and-tumble body stature admired and possessed by my husky pioneer stepfather. I must have been hypertensive and always in his way, for my memories of his shouting, "Get out of my way!" are vivid. In planting time Pa had brought Mother to the farm to help him, and for some unknown reason I was there. Pa took me to a sagebrush patch next to the trees at the foot of the mountain, handed me a grubbing hoe, and told me to clear the plot of sagebrush while he and Mother worked in the field. I hoed at the brush for hours, trying to cut it, with no more success than trying to cut down an oak tree with a hacksaw.

Tough sage wood never yielded to the hoe. I dropped the hoe and moped my way to the farmhouse, now sparsely furnished for temporary use. I stopped by the creek for a time, watching water spiders walk on water and minnows swim in quiet pools. There I loitered in peaceful unawareness of communication with nature. Then I went to the house.

In the living room Pa had some blocks of wood for chairs to sit on at the table. To while away the day I got a hammer and a large spike from Pa's carpenter shop and drove the spike halfway into the center of a wood-block chair. At home that night Pa, about to sit on the chair, broke into a fit of anger and demanded that I pull out the spike. I worked for days and never would have pulled the spike had not Mother told me, clandestinely, how to bend the spike over with the hammer, then pound it round and round until it loosened in its hole. It must have been a day or two after I got the spike out that it happened.

Pa Durney had had no experience with children before he married Mother. He knew men, strong mountain men and women hardened in struggle, strengthened in labor, iron-muscled, physical, courageous, and competitive. In this world of brawn he led the way. In quickness his mind and body coordinated.

Big Dick Kearsley, who exchanged work with Pa for years and admired him, said, "Pete was a good man—worth two men in work—honest an' clean—more of a scholar than me. Had one bad fault. He hadn't learnt to harness his temper, an' when he lost it, all hell broke loose—cursed like a sailor."

It was true. Thwarted, his anger boiled up like water on molten lead into a steam force of power. He must have been born with a surplus of yellow bile. He went mad at times with anger. He would beat his stubborn horse, Old Bell, while Mother wrung her hands in outrage, afraid to interfere lest the whip fall on her.

Pa and Ma came from the field one day to find that their pesky child had left the sage-clearing job again, had come to the house, got tools out of the shop, and left them lying in the grass. Pa's boiler blew. Never did he touch me with his hand or foot, but he lashed me with his tongue. Mother, incendiary herself, heard his shouts at me and began to defend me.

"Shut your damn mouth," he yelled.

She ignored him and spoke in stronger and crisper epithets.

He picked up the axe where I had left it and, carrying it toward the shop, flashed fire in his dark eyes, and through his black mustache he said, "If you don't shut your God-damn mouth, I'll mash your face in." The threatened violence did not emerge in reality. It emerged only in my terrorized fear.

It must have been later that evening that the second round of the verbal battle occurred. In the storage cells of my memory is a record of the clashing of sword-sharp, steel-strong words of two formidable foes—and I the cause. Mother's hair, shaken loose from the bob, flying in the air like a shawl, arms swinging, voices ringing flickered the flame in the coal-oil lamp. I hid and trembled in fear. At Pa's loud, profane words Mother retreated to the bedroom, slammed the door, and locked it. The madman kicked out the panel of the door and broke in.

When the voices from the bedroom softened, I heard my own breathing. I waited. I held my breath and listened. I trembled. I listened. I heard quiet voices. My fear subsided and at length, exhausted, I went to bed in my cot there in the living room.

The next morning Pa and Ma spoke courteously to each other in necessary communication.

After breakfast Mother took me in the buggy and went to our home in town.

In the month or two that followed Pa stayed alone on his farm and Mother in her home in town. A tone of quiet sorrow pervaded our home, for Mother constantly wiped tears from her cheeks in quiet emotion. Pa came to the house once. He would not come in, just handed Mother a bag of oranges, saying, "These are for my little girl," and left. As he drove away, Mother put her hand over her eyes, ran into her bedroom, and shut the door.

HAY HARVEST

On the fifth day of July alfalfa was in bloom and ready to harvest. It was then that Peter Durney, Big Dick Kearsley, and Frank Parsons joined forces to exchange work and harvest hay, for an efficient hay crew consisted of four men and four boys—two men pitching hay, and filling wagons in the field, three boys driving teams to bring hay from the field to the stackyard, one man operating the hay nets and derrick to unload the hay, a derrick boy to drive the horse that lifted hay out of the wagons onto the stack, and a man to stack the hay. After the alfalfa was mowed, raked, and piled in small piles on the field, this crew could stack the yield of ten acres, about twenty tons, in one stack each day.

At sunrise on the morning of July 5th, two men driving horses, each on mowing machines of the standard size, entered Big Dick Kearsley's hay field, and by sunset they had mowed twenty acres. The next day one man with one horse on a hay rake gathered all the hay that had been cut the day before by two mowers into windrows and into rough piles. Men with pitchforks followed the hay rake, making piles neat for gathering.

Thirsty, perspiring men in a stacking crew in July must have water to drink. At the Kearsley farm the water supply came from an irrigation ditch taken out of Trail Creek that supplied culinary water and water for livestock along its route. Peter Durney, as he drank, said, "Dishwater-warm, putrid water from this drizzle in the ditch—we are drinking typhoid germs."

Prophetic words were these, for shortly Peter and two sixteen-year-old boys, Hite Koyle and Jim Parsons, fell victims of the fever. Learning that her husband was ill, Mother went to the farm to nurse him.

"A hell of a time to get sick," Peter said to his wife. "A hell of a time—right in the middle of haying. Our lucerne will go to seed and dry on the stem."

After work a few days later Dick Kearsley came to see Peter. "We finished my hay today," he said.

"Who did you get to help?" asked Peter, "—to take the place of us sick ones?"

"Two of Ed's boys to drive the wagons," Dick answered. "The youngest, that kid, Ben, is a bad skinner—too young and weak, but he tries, and we get along. Got Jim Shaw to heave hay—damn good pitcher—not as good as you, but good."

"A bad time to get sick," Peter said.

"Don't worry," Dick said. "We're starting Parson's hay now—we'll be in yours while it's still in bloom—weather's good—we're only two–three days behind schedule."

"A hell of a time to be sick," Peter said.

"Any time is a hell of a time to be sick," said Dick. "It could'a been me, any or all of us. We're boilin' our drinking water now. Damn stupid of us not to do it before."

Later, in early August, after Mother had taken Peter's temperature, she said, "Your fever is down this morning—only a hundred and one degrees. You will be glad to know that two men with mowing machines are in the east field cutting our hay."

"Help me up, Eliza," he said. "Let me look out the window a minute."

"You are weak," she said.

"Weak and sick—Lord, help me. Never been sick before."

She helped him into a chair by the window.

"I'd like the window open," he said, "—to hear the machines."

She raised the window and propped the sash up with a ruler. They could hear the hay knives humming through the guards.

After a time Peter spoke. "Dr. Keith says it will be three months before I can work again. I'll beat that time—I'll beat it. With God's help I'll beat it."

"With God's help," she said.

Each week during Pa's illness Dr. Keith visited him. She handled her bay mare like a professional horseman when she drove around the country delivering babies and administering to the needs of sick people. Often I watched her as she arrived, sitting erect in the buggy, holding the lines tight in one hand like a teacher with a yardstick. She said "Whoa" loud and low, got out in decisive action, hitched her horse to the post, took her black bag, and walked in big steps to the house. No violet by a mossy dell, this lady, more a sturdy cedar by a rocky cliff. Mother respected her professionalism.

She brought quinine for the fever and advised Mother on nursing care and diet for the patient and on protection of family members from typhoid infection.

For six weeks Peter Durney fought the fever. There were voices in the house—fever, fever, fever sounded everywhere. Fever is up—a hundred four—quinine and sleep—fever is down—a hundred two—strength is waning. Where are the muscles? Where the flesh? Can skin and bones survive?

Dr. Keith's last visit was on August 31st. She advised my mother: "The disease has nearly run its course. The fever will break now. As you know, he is very weak—wasted away. His digestive system is eaten up. The fever-breaking time is danger time. Take his temperature often. If it falls far below normal, give him this medicine as directed. Keep him warm. Continue regular diet and care. If he lives the first few days after the fever breaks, his chances for survival are good."

Then came a night when I was awakened from worriless and dreamless sleep to find Mother shaking me gently. She said, "Pa is sick and like to die—so very sick. Get up and kneel by the bed and pray with me. Plead with Heavenly Father to save Pa's life." I got up, knelt by the bed with her. She said, "You pray in silence and I in silence."

When we stood up again, I heard Mother sobbing. I got in bed after she left and tried to stay awake and pray more, but soon fell asleep.

Pa was alive the next morning. No thought entered my mind other than that God had granted our requests. Neighbors came, and that afternoon I was playing on the swing with Delilah Wardle, laughing happily, when I saw men carrying a bed out of the house. Sensing something wrong, I ran to the house. Mother and the family were quietly crying. I looked around. Areatha said softly, "Pa is dead." I ran over to where Mother sat. She put ner arm around me, said nothing, just cried, and I cried with her. After a while Mother said, "It is God's will, he is . . ." and her voice fell in silence.

THE FARM MORTGAGE

When a life insurance salesman tried to sell Pa Durney an insurance policy he, like many skeptics of his day, told the agent, "I would not tempt Satan by gambling on my life." He had great faith in his own longevity. A good financier, he also believed that it takes money to make money. That is why he arranged to mortgage his farm. It put him into a snit after he signed the contract, and Mother into a long period of stress after his death.

Holding a letter in his hand one day, Pa burst into a fit of temper. "That son of a bitch, George Young—I'm going to smash his fat face in."

Startled in fright, my mother said, "What under heaven has brought on this raging violence?"

"That lying bastard has cheated me," he said.

The shock of those profane, explosive words sank deep into my eight-year-old mind. Even then I must have felt the incongruity of those words coming out of the mouth from which I had heard humble prayers. Not until I matured did I comprehend the cause and significance of my stepfather's anger, nor did I dream at that time of the result and the interminable impression it would leave on my mind.

Through George Young's office in Driggs, Peter Durney had applied for and received approval of a mortgage on his farm, the principal of $500 to be delivered on May 1st. The letter that Peter received that day said that the money would not be delivered until November. Furthermore, interest at 10 percent would be charged from the date of the mortgage, and then—the deepest cut of the usurer's hatchet—the first year's interest would be withheld from the principal. Peter would receive only $450. Of this he had not been apprised. At this unfair contract Peter rebelled and demanded cancellation of the mortgage contract. George Young refused to cancel, the refusal based, he said, on rules set down by the mortgage company he represented.

Now, caught in the vise, Peter bought farm machinery that spring with his promise to pay when the mortgage money came that fall.

In August of that year Peter died, leaving Mother with the burden. On November 1st the money, $450, came and went for debts. The weight of that mortgage seemed to multiply in misfortune for my mother through twelve long years of frugal widowhood. We six children felt the burden. Much of commerce in the valley was done by barter. Gold and silver, the major mediums of exchange, eluded us. A twenty-dollar gold coin looked as big and bright as the sun. Thus Mother would say, "We must save money for the mortgage." Actually she meant money for interest on the mortgage: $50 due each year. To pay the principal stayed as far from her mind as paying the principal of the national debt stays from the minds of politicians. We all felt the pressure. Money for the mortgage! Even the logs in the house seemed to whisper, "Save the farm! Get money for the mortgage!"

The burden shadowed the Durney farm until Mother married again and the debt was paid in 1921.

"A mortgage," said Mother, "is a dangerous incubus, a leech that sucks the blood of its victims."

3

No Place Like Home, 1905–1916

AREATHA CHENEY

I t was milking time in the evening. Areatha took me by the hand and we walked down into the field to bring in the cows. She carried me across the ditch, for it was too wide for my short legs to span. The hay had been stacked and now the milk cows pastured in the hay fields. The sun sank near the western mountains as the crispness of evening breezes in the yellowing aspen trees fluttered the leaves in sounds of soft percussion. Our black dog, Night, followed us, flitting here and there following some scent or other.

Areatha, with the help of Night, rounded up the cows. The big, long-horned bull with the herd grazed with one cow at the periphery down by the fence. Areatha sent Night down to bring in these two stragglers. I broke away and ran, following the dog. The bull, aroused by the disturbance and angered at the dog nipping at his heels, must have seen me as an enemy colleague of the dog and as a better target for revenge. He came with head down, bounding and bellowing toward me. I ran! I ran hard! I ran very hard! The bull and I reached the edge of Warm Creek at the same time. I stopped and turned, almost as fearful of the water as of the bull. There I met eye to eye those big, bulging, beastly eyes of the angry bull. I saw those huge, sharp horns circling my head. I felt the force of dragon breath on my legs.

Then it happened! It happened so very quickly. The bull withdrew, striking me slightly at the temple with his horn as if by accident. It appeared that he could have been an animal trained to frighten and not to injure.

Only then did I become aware of Areatha standing back a few steps yelling and vigorously swinging a stick. The bull turned and looked at her, as if to decide on strategy. Then he shook his head a little as if to say, "Oh, what the hell!" and off he trotted toward the retreating cows. Areatha picked me up, hugged me, examined me, found a little scratch at my temple, kissed me, and cried a little. As I heard her rapid breathing subside, she put me down and we followed the cows to the barn. As we neared home I lagged behind. Areatha took me in her arms again. "Poor child," she said. "You are still trembling, trembling like quaking-asp leaves."

BEDBUGS AND BACTERIA

In those years before World War I, ours was a life of plenty—plenty of kindness, hopes, dreams, neighbors, relatives, friends, work, noise, winter, sickness, and pests.

While Mother did not have the purchasing power to buy first-class necessities, she had the willpower to be a first-class human being and to trust her children to follow. She had a prophet's foresight and a philosopher's insight. She saw the corrupting effect of bedbugs on both beds and people. A bedbug bite was a bite on the moral fiber of human dignity. Dirt was bad company. Bedbugs meant dirty beds. Dirty beds could breed dirty thoughts, and dirty thoughts led to dirty deeds. Therefore, Mother declared war on bedbugs. She not only declared extermination war on those dirty little devils, she practiced preventive measures against all pests.

Ours was a log house covered now with siding on the outside and lined with lumber on the inside. Over the lumber a thin, coarsely woven cloth called "factory" was stretched and shower-tacked, and onto that was pasted the decorative wallpaper. Yet, despite this wallpaper covering, Mother would feel something at night just after she went to bed. She would scratch, feel around, and find a tomato seed. Then she would get up, strike a match with her free hand, light the coal-oil lamp, and look at the tomato seed to find that it was a bedbug. That was disaster! She would get all the family out of bed for a bedbug hunt. She would hold the lamp while we rolled out the bed and searched the wall, not only for bedbugs but for any hole in the paper through which a bug could come. We would give every quilt, blanket, pillow, sheet, and the straw mattress microscopic examination. We would search the frontside, the backside, the underside, and the topside of the wooden bedstead for bugs and for holes and cracks that might be breeding spots. She knew bedbugs were at home in wood, which inspired her complete abhorrence for the log house and the wooden bedstead. When Mama prayed, "Keep us from all harm," I knew that she meant bedbugs.

Annual housecleaning in those days amounted to a complete purification ritual designed to eradicate from our domain everything evil, from rats to black widow spiders to bedbugs to the unseen and unseeable communicable disease germs and viruses. Every room got the treatment, and last of all came the living room. First, we took out all the furniture, then pulled the carpet tacks to loosen the wall-to-wall carpeting, then dragged the carpet out and hung it over the clotheslines. Mama would hand us a broom and say, "Beat it." We would beat it until all the dust was out of it and onto us, lay down the broom, and say, "Finished." Before the dust settled, however, Mama would perceive a lull in the percussion area of the housecleaning symphony and call from the house, "Beat it some more." This was repeated ad lib.

Next we would remove the straw padding that had been under the carpet, now ground fine, sweep and mop the floor, then string wires across the room to prepare for fumigation. Fumigation would kill anything, be it as big as a rat or small enough for a billion to reside under a pinhead. We opened the closets, arranged clothes loosely, put the furniture and carpet back in, opened drawers, unfolded blankets, exposed everything to permit the fumes of formaldehyde to penetrate possible hiding places for the egg or seed of any living organism. We would shut the stove draft, close the damper, shut all windows, plug the .22 bullet hole in a windowpane, and plug the keyhole with an eraser. Then Mama would spray the liquid formaldehyde on the sheets strung over the wires in the room. As the stench began to sting our noses we would exit, close and lock the doors, and leave the deadly fumes to perform the feat of sterilization.

Then came the reconstruction period. Sometimes Mother would get so tied up with cutting, pasting, and hanging paper that she would forget to feed us, and we would get so hungry that we would eat the paste. Next came getting and preparing the straw for the padding under the carpet, stretching and tacking the carpet down, washing windows, hanging blinds and curtains, and, finally, arranging the furniture.

Now that the ritual was over, Mother took a leave of absence from worry about bedbags or the plague. She worried only about stiff hands, sore feet, backache, bloodshot eyes, and upset stomach.

Grandma Rice

Grandma Rice lived in a one-room log hut across from the baseball diamond, about as far away from our house as a batter could bat a ball. After her husband died, her children had moved her from her ranch to town near neighbors. We called her Grandma because she was old and acted like a grandma, kind and loving and interested in us. Her children with families lived on farms about four miles west of town in Cedron Ward and came to visit their mother only about once in a fortnight. Grandma needed friends and Mother supplied the need.

We all watched out for Grandma. Mother instructed us, "Be good to her. She is such a lovely soul. Left alone by the hurrying world, she can't work, her eyes are dim, she can't see, she can't read, she can't sew. All she can do is think, and the products of her mind—facts, memories, dreams—become tangled."

One wintry night Naomi came in just after dark and said, "Grandma doesn't have her light on."

Mother quickly put on her coat and went to check. Shortly she came home and reported, "Grandma is all right. Her lamp flickered out and she couldn't find the matches. She is feeble. I fear her life will soon flicker out."

Mother instructed us children, "Whenever you go to pick up the mail or to the store, stop and talk with Grandma."

One day as I went toward her house, I saw her come out the door dressed in her dark, long flannel dress covered in front with an apron which she held up in her hand as if she carried something in it. As I approached her, I saw her gray hair against her withered face and her palsied fingers throwing crumbs out of her apron to feed the birds.

"Hello, Grandma," I said. "I'll go on so I won't frighten the birds away."

"I don't see good," she said, "but I know you are Nervy's good boy. You can talk to me, the birds will come later."

One day, sitting in our living room after wearying her way to our house, she said, "Nobody around at my house anymore. Alone in the house listenin', hearin' nothin' but the logs crack in the walls, the clock tick, the wood spit in the stove, the wind whisper past the door, and a cow bawl in the distance. Sometimes I want to go out and yell at the cliff just to hear the echo."

"I should visit you more often," my mother said. "Tell me, Grandma, what have you heard lately?"

"What have I heerd?" she repeated. "Let me see . . . I heerd . . . I don't remember whether I heerd it or dremt it . . . but a star or a comet or somethin' or other is goin' to shoot by or hit us . . . I think . . . with a fire stringin' behind it like a horse's tail. Have you heerd that, Nervy?"

"Yes," Mother said. "You didn't dream it, Grandma. The *Denver Post* says that Halley's Comet can be seen next Monday about four o'clock in the morning."

Grandma Rice smiled.

THE FACTS OF LIFE

My stepfather had died, and my mother had called me, at ten, the man of the house. I slopped pigs, fed chickens, gathered eggs, and milked cows. I felt big until Eugene cut me down one day. I'll tell you about it.

The cows were acting up in the corral that morning, so I drove Old Bossy over to the Bagleys' to the bull. Eugene Lauritzen joined me at the north forty and helped me drive the cow. Fred Bagley opened the bull pen and let

Bossy in. Eugene and I watched. "It's July tenth today," I said. I counted on my fingers, "August, one, September, two, October, three . . ." and on to April. "The calf will be born on April tenth. I'll put that down in Mama's record book."

"Nine months—same length of time as it takes for a baby," Eugene said.

"As a baby?" I asked, astonished. "As a real baby?"

"Sure," he said. "Don't you know about that?"

I stood in shock.

"Where do you think you came from?" he asked.

"From heaven," I said.

"How do you think you got here?"

"An angel or a—I don't know," I said.

"You came out of your mother like a calf comes. Your mother carried you inside like a cow carries a calf," he explained.

I was astonished and speechless. After a pause I asked, "How—how did—what started me?"

"Your father," he said.

"It is not like that!" I said in disgust. "Be dirty like—my mother wouldn't. She—"

"But she did! You are here!"

A whirlwind of thought arose in my brain. Then I asked, "If I came out, how did I get out?"

"Have you seen a calf born?" he asked.

"Yes."

"Well—then you know!"

"Does a man have to do *that* to a woman to get a baby?" I asked.

" 'Course," he said.

"How can they do it?"

"Don't you know a thing? How can you be so stupid?" he said.

"I don't like it," I said. "It's not nice! It's dirty! It's vulgar."

He laughed. "You're a child."

"Could I have a baby—make a girl have—?" I asked.

"Naw! Ya got to wait 'til puberty—'til your voice changes."

"You do it with your voice?" I asked.

"No. It's when ya get hair on your face and have to shave—when ya get to be a man like me," he said. "I could, I'm old enough." He was emphasizing his low voice.

How could a child who had been conditioned in idealism, shielded from mundane truth, bring compatibility out of such incompatibility? I went home that day with a troubled mind. What Eugene said seemed so right and yet so disgustingly wrong. I had heard about women being big with child, yet paid it no heed. I thought that night most about my mother. She had deceived me. I could not think of her and other people being like animals.

Mother sat reading that night, and I sat on the floor looking at her quizzically. I can't tell her what I know—how bad she has been—I'll ask Eugene more—I'll not ask her—I'll ask him if . . . I was looking at her, not seeing her there, but seeing a creation of my troubled mind.

Mother saw me. "Why are you staring at me so strangely," she said, "as if you hated me?"

The question disturbed me.

"Have I done something? Hurt your feelings?" she continued.

"Yes," I said.

"Tell me. What have I done?"

"I can't tell you," I said.

"Come on—tell me—I can't think of anything I've done today to hurt you."

"It's not today," I said.

"What—for heaven's sake—could I have done to you to upset you?" she asked.

"It's not to me," I said.

"Did you see me do it?" she asked.

"No!" I answered.

"Have I ever done it before?" she asked.

"*Six* times you've done it," I said.

"Did you see me do it six times?" she asked.

"No. I didn't see you do it at all," I said.

"Who told you I did it? Who did see me?" she asked.

"Nobody saw you do it," I said.

"If nobody saw me do it, how do you know I did it?" she argued.

"I just realized it out," I said.

"What a puzzle you are!" she said. "Maybe you will tell me what it is tomorrow." With that she took up her book to read again.

This confrontation I had with one of the paradoxes of life kept flashing into my consciousness for days and days as I explored the area of the process of birth. A maturing child with big ears, I listened to the girl talk of my older sisters and mother. I pondered more on both intellectual and crude talk of men. I asked Eugene and older boys intimate questions, all the time avoiding dialogue with Mother. One day, however, a week or so later, she must have sensed my struggle with the oxymoronic world. She said, "Lovemaking in marriage is a thing of enjoyment and beauty, leading to the great joy of becoming parents."

I did not question her, but continued to wrestle with the incongruity of the mansions of love being in the place of excrement.

AUNT MARY

Aunt Mary lived across the street from us—dear Aunt Mary. She was Mother's sister, twenty years older, and like a grandmother to us. She came across the street to our house nearly every day, and sometimes more than once. Her visits were short, just long enough to deliver a bit of news or to inquire about someone's health or about some project someone had in progress. Aunt Mary's long, high-necked dresses made of dark flannel spoke of utility, not art. Ostentation, affectation, or pretense were as foreign to her as etiquette to a pig. A pioneer she was, full of integrity, strong and sturdy, no pushover blown about by every wind of doctrine.

One day I stood in the kitchen where Mother and Aunt Mary were having their chitchat. Suddenly my sister Naomi burst into the room in a fit of terror.

"Mama," she shouted, "I'm bleeding—I'm bleeding inside," and she burst into tears.

Aunt Mary said to Mother, "Gracious sakes, Nervy, haven't you told her about that? You should have prepared her for it."

"It's all right, Naomi," Mother said. "It comes to girls. Don't cry."

"Then I won't bleed to death?" Naomi said.

"Come into the bedroom," Mother said. "I'll tell you about it."

They went away, leaving me and Aunt Mary alone.

I said, "I know what it is, Aunt Mary. Naomi's got puberty."

Aunt Mary laughed. "Is that so?" she said. "What's puberty?"

"It's something she's got to get before she has a baby."

"Is that so?" said Aunt Mary. "Land-a-mercy, where did you learn that?"

"From the cows," I said. "They do just like people do."

"Cows don't talk! They can't tell you," she said. "Did you learn it from the street?"

"Naw. Streets don't talk," I said. "I just know more than Naomi does. She's dumb. She doesn't know about puberty and something that girls have . . . and how babies . . . where babies . . ."

"Do you think Naomi is going to have a baby?" she inquired.

"No. But she could now if—"

"I declare," said Aunt Mary, "and you learned it from the cows."

"It's like this," I said, "If . . . if she got married and had . . ."

"That's enough," broke in Aunt Mary. "You are too big for your britches."

That night at the supper table I asked, "Is it bad to be too big for your britches?"

"Did someone tell you you are?" Mother asked.

"Yes, Aunt Mary did."

"If Aunt Mary said you are, you are."

"Is it bad?" I pleaded.

"Not if Aunt Mary said it," Mother answered.

Pleasant Sherman

Areatha Cheney had grown up and become a beautiful girl, well endowed with feminine charm. An Easter queen she was that spring, bonneted, corseted, buttoned, frilled, and perfumed. She attracted the attention of the charming piano pounder who followed the beat of the stomping foot of the fiddler in the dance orchestra. This piano player added spice to the dance music at times by strumming the guitar, banjo, or mandolin. His name was Pleasant Sherman—Plez we called him—and a pleasant man he was. Sandy-complexioned, he had a perpetual smile and well-groomed, light red hair. A modified Texas drawl in his speech embroidered with singular colloquialisms, and a courtesy in his behavior born of natural shyness, made him unique. Areatha enjoyed his attention. She enjoyed his sonorous southern drawl. "Y'all's lookin' right smart, Missie—right smart," he would say. She enjoyed his careful attention when he said, "Beggin' ya pa'dun, Missie, but betta ya move over so the mare won't splash mud on ya fancy duds."

Pleasant Sherman's shyness abated as he pursued his lady love. Love turns a shy kitten into a bold cat. After a year of ardent pursuit of Areatha's love, after a sincere study of her religious faith and his conversion, and after she succumbed hopelessly to his devotion and reciprocated it with loyal affection, they planned a spring marriage.

To finance his marriage, Pleasant spent the winter pursuing his sometime trade of trapping, a trade rapidly becoming extinct in America. Trapping fur-bearing animals was a winter occupation, for that was the time when fur grew tight and thick. Furs brought good profits. Plez had learned the trapping business from his father. He knew the animals' characteristics, their habitats, their foods, their hiding places. The furs most profitable—beaver, mink, and bear—were scarce, but a good trapper could get an occasional remnant of them. His chief game, however, were martin, muskrat, and coyote.

With a hunting knife, a single-shot pistol, and a backpack of traps, food, and furs to keep warm, he went on cross-country skis of his own make into the Teton Mountain Range of the Targhee National Forest on the southwest boundary area of the valley. A natural woodsman, he had learned the art of finding fuel and building a fire to fight the frost and that of recognizing danger signals of violent nature—the storm, the wind, the avalanche. He knew well the work of skinning the captured animals while still warm to use the body heat of his prey to keep his naked hands from freezing.

Home from following the trapping lines, Plez Sherman would lay out his hides to dry, hang up his trapping gear, limber up his fingers, toughened and stiffened by the cold, and join the orchestra in the dance hall to pound music on the piano—tunes like "After the Ball" for a waltz, or "Turkey in the Straw" for a square or a round dance.

The trapping business never yielded better returns for Plez Sherman than it did in the winter of 1911–12 and courtship never filled him and his betrothed with more joy. Areatha would come home from a ride in his cutter, drawn by a lively white buggy horse, and sing, "The winter king holds reverie tonight" and "I can be happy forever with just one beau." By spring Plez had earned enough money to finance the wedding. He bought a new buggy and drove with his betrothed fifty miles to Rexburg. There they boarded the train for Salt Lake City, where they took their wedding vows in the famed six-towered Salt Lake temple.

Areatha never looked so beautiful to me, nor Plez so handsome, as they did that June day when they drove away to be married. Mother cried! Areatha shed a tear or two as they waved good-bye.

In Salt Lake City the bride, with her spouse—the trapper, musician, lover—spent money that had literally come out of his hides to buy furniture to ship home to equip the new cabin he had built on the homestead in the foothills south of the String Canal.

SUMMER VISITORS

In that most perplexing age when my pants legs rapidly got too short for my legs and my voice played yodeling tricks on my communication, my mother received a letter from a relative—a shirttail relative. She was my deceased stepfather's half sister, whom Mother had met once long ago. The short letter put Mother and our whole family into a fever of speculation, for the letter said, "We are going to come and visit you for a month. Look for two tramps and a bum." Aside from the aunt and her husband, who could the third one be—a friend, a son, a daughter?

When Mother and I met the train on which these relatives arrived, we had no trouble identifying them. I looked for and found two tramps and a bum. The man carried a bag, a seamless wheat sack full of clothes. A boy—oh, curses, about my age—carried a broken-down, beat-up suitcase tied together with a rope. Aunt Matilda, I concluded at a glance, had inherited her clothes from her grandma. Though the June heat beat down, she wore a

coat designed for a girl of twenty with a waistline fitted to the mold of
steel-ribbed corsets, buttoned now by necessity only above the waistline.
Heavy black stockings circled in sagging rings above her high-topped button
shoes. She looked like a leftover relic of the nineties. Her husband, yielding
to the heat of the summer day, had removed his coat and carried it along
with the bag of clothes. Wide galluses, holding up his pants and pressing his
white shirt to his ample rotundity, showed a border of sweat through the
shirt. Black arm bands kept his long sleeves from covering his hands. The
boy looked no less antiquated. Long ago, a couple months at least, I had
abandoned knickers for more manly long pants, but this gangling boy, fully
as tall as I, wore knickers, outgrown and ugly, so tight and short that the
waistband rode his hip bone in order for the strap to buckle at the knee.

These were my poor relations. When I later encountered Charles Lamb's
essay, "Poor Relations," I cried with delight at his prolific descriptive exposi-
tion on characteristics of this phenomenon:

> A Poor Relation is the most irrelevant thing in nature, a piece of impertinent
> correspondency, an odious approximation—a haunting conscience—a preposter-
> ous shadow, lengthening in the noontide of our prosperity—an unwelcome
> remembrancer—a perpetually reoccurring mortification—a drain upon your
> purse, a more intolerable drain upon your pride. . . . a stain on your blood—a
> blot on your scutcheon—a rent in your garment—a mote in your eye—a triumph
> to your enemy, an apology to your friends—the one thing not needful.

We at our home knew poverty. I had to make one pencil last from school
opening until Christmas. On Railroad Celebration Day I smelled the popcorn rather than bought it, and on the Fourth of July I made one five-cent
box of firecrackers last a week after the holiday. But I did not have to wear
funny old clothes. I knew now that I was not poor.

With this boy—this oddity—at my home I avoided my friends as long as I
could, and each night I lay in insomnia lasting on and on up to ten minutes
trying to determine how I could keep this cousin a secret. Each day I found
him more intolerable. He stood at the heels of a horse. I said, "Don't stand
there; he may kick you. Stand at his head."

"I daresn't," he said. "He'll bite me."

"Anybody knows that a horse doesn't bite," I said.

"He'll kick me with his front foot," he said.

I couldn't answer. I could only laugh. I saddled and bridled the horse, got
on, and said, "Get on behind me." He started to get on from the wrong side.
The horse shied. "Don't you know a thing?" I said. "You've got to get on
from the other side."

He asked me silly questions: "Will the cow bite?" "Does the bull give
milk?" "Why do you have to milk a cow from only one side?" "Why does the

cow kick forward with her hind foot when you milk her?" One night as I milked a cow and he stood near, not looking, I shot a squirt of milk from the cow's teat into his ear. He jumped, turned around as he wiped his ear, and said, "I didn't know that a cow would squirt milk at a person she don't like."

I smothered my laughter and said, "Oh, they do, just like a skunk."

One day I told him that his hair was as long as a girl's and that my mother could cut it for him. He said, "I got my hair cut by a barber once in Salt Lake—by a real barber that had a turning barber pole."

"You mean that red and white striped barber pole?" I said.

"Yes, like peppermint candy."

"Barber poles never turn," I said. "You were dizzy."

We argued until dark. At that time I knew that he was the stupidest kid I had ever seen.

On Saturday we could go up to the pond in the trees and swim. We had just started away on the horse when James said, "Do you have swimming suits?"

I said, "Just boys there. Don't need any."

He said, "You can't swim naked. They'd see you, and girls might come."

"They won't."

"Why won't they?"

"Because they know we are naked. Boys and girls are different.

"Do you have a swimming suit at home?" I asked.

"No," he said, "I use a flour sack. You cut two holes in the bottom for your legs and pin it over the shoulders and it makes a good suit."

Boys were already at the pond when we arrived, some in the water and some sitting naked on the bank. I quickly pulled off my clothes and waded into the water slowly to get adjusted to the cool water. James stood without moving.

"Why don't your cousin come in?" yelled a boy. "Can't he swim?"

"He can swim," I yelled back.

"Is he afraid of cold water?" the boy shouted.

"No" I said, "he's afraid to get naked."

"Hey," yelled another to James, "what's the matter? Are you a girl or something?"

That insult made James forget all about the swimming suit. I could see anger in his face. In no time he was naked as a baby bird. He ran to the pond and made a leaping dive into the deepest hole, came up, shook his head, and swam like a fish across the pond. He didn't get angry when they ducked him and he didn't gripe about the cold water. Before the day was over he sat on the bank naked with the boys, telling them about the big heated swimming pool and how you could really dive well from a diving board.

"What's a diving board?" they asked.

That day with his clothes off, I almost liked James.

On Saturday Mother said, "Tomorrow you will take James to Sunday School."

"He looks funny," I said.

"You will not look funny," she said.

"I will with him," I said.

"He's a nice boy, you know," she said.

I knew that I could not, I must not, take this peculiarity to Sunday School, for there Florence would see me with him. I loved Florence secretly with the deepest abstract love in all the world. She was so beautiful . . . and so nice . . . and so sweet! She would turn sour on me if she saw James. I had written her name in the mud when I watered the garden and in my heart and I wanted it to stay. If Florence saw this long-haired cousin with his bummy clothes, she would desert me. The thought was insufferable. I determined that I would not taint my blood with this poison.

I argued with Mother. I tried everything. At last I determined to be sick Sunday morning. I filled my stomach with raw turnips, which had worked before, but this time it didn't work. Nothing worked. Try as I might, I couldn't turn pale and I couldn't vomit. I had to take my yoke upon me and bear my burden in desperate silence.

At Sunday School assembly I sat by James in laconic taciturnity, mum and numb in embarrassment. In class the teacher said, "Thomas, will you introduce your cousin?"

I sat tongue-tied, thinking, He's not my cousin—I won't claim him. My breath would hardly come. I started tugging at a buttonhole in my coat.

"Please, Thomas," said the teacher.

"James . . ." I hesitated.

"Stand up," she called, "you and your guest."

Stand up, I thought. Damn it (only God would know I thought it and He would understand), they'll see every inch of his knickers—and me with him—damn it! Damn it! Damn it!

I stood with James and felt like Lady Godiva on her horse, wishing no one would look. "It's James," I said, "James Barlow from Salt Lake City."

We sat down and the teacher began to question James.

I ducked my head. Yet in time I became interested in what James was saying. I saw the big tabernacle with a roof like a turtle shell, the big pipe organ he had heard, the temple with six towers, the Seagull Monument, the Eagle Gate, and Saltair where you could float on the water.

After Sunday School Florence and Carrie, her girl friend, ran over to where we were. "We want to meet your cousin," Florence said to me. "Isn't it great to live in Salt Lake City and just know everything?"

"Meet James," I said. "James, Florence and Carrie."

"I like you, James," Florence said—along with other unimportant things. Then she asked, "James, do you have a garden of beautiful flowers in Salt Lake City?"

"No, we don't," he answered.

"Thomas does," she said, "and he brings me pretty bouquets. Isn't he nice?"

At home later I asked James, "Is it a long walk from your house to the tabernacle to hear the organ?"

"I don't walk. I ride."

"You don't have a horse," I said.

"I ride the streetcar."

"Does it run on electricity like in San Francisco?"

" 'Course."

"How does it get electricity when electricity comes in wires?"

"It runs on a wire."

"Can't run on a wire," I said. "It runs on the ground."

"A little wheel runs on a wire up above and the electricity is grounded on the rails."

"Does it run on a railroad track?" I asked.

"Sure."

"Electricity grounded? What do you mean?"

"It means . . . it means . . . why are you so dumb? You don't know beans!"

"I know beans better'n you do, but I don't know streetcars."

He laughed and I laughed. "It's like this," he said. "Electricity comes into the streetcar through the wire and it ain't—it isn't goin' ta turn the motor unless it can get out."

"Why?" I asked.

"Nobody knows why. It's like water. Water won't turn a generator if it can't run through."

"I got it," I said, "the electricity comes out of the wire, through the motor in the streetcar, out into the rails, and into the ground—grounded."

"You got it—finally," he said, "slow . . . slow, not fast like Edison."

"Edison wasn't fast," I said. "I read about him. His teacher said he couldn't learn—and he did a dumb thing, tried to set on eggs to hatch them like a hen."

"He did not."

"He did too. I read it. He was experimenting. If a hen could do it, he knew he could."

"But I know he had his head on straight," James said emphatically in anger.

"Sure," I said, "I know. Sure—he had his head tied on so his brains wouldn't ravel out, but at school his teacher thought he was a numbskull—but he wasn't."

Later one day we were riding up Pole Canyon when James asked, "How many warts you got?"

"None."

"I got five on this hand," he said as he held it up, "three on this hand, and one on my neck. See."

"I know how to kill 'em. It's easy," I said.

He was all ears.

"Take a potato, cut it in half, rub the potato juice on each wart, then bury the potato, and when it rots the warts will die."

"Fooey," he said with a look of disappointment.

"It works," I argued. "It works. I did it and it did. Look, no warts," I said, holding out my hands.

"What if the potato grows? Then you would have more warts," he said.

"You bury it deep so it can't, stupid."

"That's all superstitch—all a—all lame-brained, witch-doctor bunk," he said.

"But I told you! I did it! It worked!" I yelled. "I played with toads and got warts and—"

"Bunko, bunko," he interrupted, "the potato didn't take 'em. They just went."

"Nothing goes away doin' nothing."

"They do too—stomachache and headache and colds and whooping cough and everything."

"Them's pains, not warts. Go ahead, keep your warts! Hold 'em tight! Let 'em grow! They're your warts! I wouldn't give you even a potato peeling to cure 'em, not if you begged me."

Suddenly we saw a skunk eating the carcass of a dead calf and forgot our anger.

Often in the evenings I could ditch James. He could play checkers with my sister, and I could read. Mr. Stephens, my schoolteacher, had loaned me the book *The Last Days of Pompeii*. Now I had come to the interesting part. James came into the room just as I finished the book. Tears must have been in my eyes, for he teased me about crying over a story.

"Nydia died," I said, "jumped overboard into the sea!"

"You liked her," he said.

"She was blind," I said.

"Is that why she jumped over?" he asked.

"She saved Glaucus and Ione from being buried in ash in Pompeii."

"Pompeii was buried in hot lava," he said.

"It was ash," I said.

"Rock out of the ground don't burn like wood," he said.

"Ash," I said, "and it darkened the sky, dead dark, dark as Tom Sawyer's cave, but Nydia had gone to the seashore before, always by feel, and she led them that could see when they had light but who in the dark could not find the way. She saved Glaucus and Ione from death."

"Why did she jump off the ship?"

"She loved Glaucus, but Glaucus loved Ione."

After a pause James said, "I read *Uncle Tom's Cabin*."

"Did you cry?" I asked.

"It was sad, but I did not cry. Men don't cry over stories."

We did not argue much during the last part of James's visit. We laughed at times and at other times talked about Salt Lake City and things in general. He said he liked the farm and he thought he would come and visit me again sometime. I told him I'd let him come if he wanted to, but I probably couldn't keep the cows from squirting milk in his ears. He laughed and laughed.

"What are you going to do when you get back to Salt Lake City?" I asked.

"I'm going to make some money."

"How?" I asked.

"From now to winter a lot of coal cars with lump coal come by our house and the locomotives stop and start fast and some lumps fall off the open cars as they move them on side tracks. I go down with our wheelbarrow and gather the coal. Pa and Grandpa pay me a penny a pound."

"What'll you do with the money?" I asked.

"Buy me some long pants and a tailor-made shirt like yours," he said.

The day came for our summer visitors to leave. At that time I thought about how nice it would be to have a twin brother. Now after weeks of talking, discussing, arguing, quarreling, and laughing, James and I were inarticulate. As we waited for the boarding of the train, Mother said, "You boys have become great friends."

"Yes," James said.

Good-byes were being said. James just looked at me, said nothing, then turned to go. I said, "James, I think your warts will go away just doing nothing."

He turned with a smile and said, "Good-bye."

As the train pulled away, I waved. For some reason I felt very sad, but I made sure I did not cry.

Uncertified Teachers, 1905–1916

WILLIAM WARDLE

William Wardle, a neighbor and an elder in the church, baptized me. I went that late November day after my eighth birthday to the Wardle home unwillingly, for at that time I disliked Will Wardle. I had a grudge against him because he pried into my affairs and had asked me a personal question. "Is it true," he had said, "that your stepfather made you eat cow manure because you played in it and got dirty?"

I answered emphatically, "He did not!" But, inarticulately, I did not say how burned-up I was that he would think I would play in manure or that my father would or could make me eat it.

However, he was nice to me and his daughter Delilah the day he baptized us—teased us, as we walked down to the creek, about being afraid of the cold water.

I had been taught about the sacredness of baptism, how it would wash away sins. But when Will Wardle said a few words, rather irreverently, in prayer and then pushed Delilah under, I felt unhappy. Delilah ran for the house in wet clothes, and I waded into the creek looking at the thin ice forming at the edge of the creek. He baptized me with dispatch as the weather demanded, and together we ran for the house. As we entered Wardle's kitchen, I shivered convulsively.

Delilah had already stripped off her wet clothes and stood naked, drying herself by the fire. I followed her father into another room where he ordered, "You go back by the fire." He pushed me out and shut the door. There I stood, compromised by a naked girl.

I had been taught never to be with a naked girl and never, never to undress before one. Delilah's older sister handed me a towel as I stood shivering, making no move toward removing my wet clothes. As Delilah put on her pants, her father entered, buttoning his shirt.

"Don't just stand there like a dunce," he said to me. "Take off those wet clothes, wipe yourself, and put on dry clothes."

"Here?" I said.

"Here," he said.

There I was newly cleansed from sin—and forced into corruption. I stripped naked before Delilah and her sister. William Wardle had led me into my first accountable sin.

Kind Uncle George

On a Sunday morning when I was about nine years old I performed an anatomic experiment. My laboratory was the Sunday School classroom. Equipment included a strong string and my finger. "Please quit playing with that string," the teacher said. But the tone of her voice sounded less than imperative, so I continued my experiment, the purpose of which was to find out all the colors the end of the index finger on my left hand would turn when a strong string was wound tightly around and around below the second knuckle. The experiment was working: my finger had turned pink, then red, and had begun to turn purple when the teacher, reaching out her long arm—six feet long at least—grabbed the end of the string and jerked. The string came off, also part of my finger. At first it did not hurt, for the tight string had anesthetized the finger. Shortly Sunday School was over, to my relief. I ran outside holding my finger behind me, for I knew it was bleeding profusely and I wanted no one to see.

When I moved away from the church and was alone, I could and did cry; tears came freely. In this condition, with bloody hands and foggy eyes, I met Uncle George and learned that he was a kind and gentle man.

Uncle George, I had been led to believe, was my most careless, most shiftless, most lazy, and most carefree uncle. He not only could fiddle while Rome burned, he could sleep while the straw mattress under him burned. I always thought that Rip Van Winkle was Uncle George's brother. His last name was Meek, and at that time I thought "meek" meant someone gentle, harmless, penniless, friendly, lethargic, and smelling of tobacco juice as he did.

I believed that Uncle George never exercised willpower because he had no will. Relatives had told me that sometime after the close of the Civil War Grandfather could have ordered George Meek at the point of a shotgun to marry his daughter, Aunt Jane. When confronted with the situation Uncle George characteristically wasted no effort; he married her—took her in a wagon some seventy miles to be married "right" in the temple at Manti.

After the marriage ceremony he bought a jug of whiskey and celebrated all the way home. He was sick every morning and soused every afternoon, submissive as a lamb in the forenoon and happy as a hyena in the afternoon. Believing his horses and wagon as invincible as himself, he purposely tried every afternoon to steer the hind wheel of his wagon to lock it with other wagons he met. Successes in life for him were few, but in this he finally succeeded. The other team and wagon proved stronger than his, however, which resulted in his arriving home with a sad young wife, an empty jug, and a three-wheeled wagon with the fourth axle supported by a drag log.

Uncle George was a good provider. He provided Aunt Jane with three sons, five daughters, and a ton of worries. He provided his family with a peck of patience and a bushel of love, not wholly unrequited. He provided them with shabby shelter, air-conditioned clothes with vents everywhere, and a hunger instinct that led them, with the help of their mother, to get food for a shaky survival. They lived on pigweed greens, thistle pickle, watermelon peel jam, bedbug currants, pork tongue, head cheese, tripe, and liver; sagebrush tea, skimmed milk, clabber, whey—and on cabbage, turnips, and Indian corn that Aunt Jane grew in her garden.

When Uncle George saw me that Sunday, alone with bloody hands and tear-filled eyes, his own eyes moistened in sympathy. He put his arm around me and said, "Ah, Sonny, ye've barked yer finger—don't cry! I'll fix her up fer ya." He took a white handkerchief out of his Levi pocket, shifted the cud in his mouth, chewed a bit, whistled a shot of juice through his teeth and yellow-edged mustache to the ground, folded the handkerchief into a bandage, carefully exhumed the well-chewed cud onto the cloth, applied the poultice to the wound, and tied it with some of my string. He did it all with skill, with sympathy, and with a heart full of fatherly love.

Regardless of the repulsion I felt for "Climax" mixed with saliva, I immediately felt the soothing effect of the poultice. Tears left my eyes as I thanked him.

At home Mama removed the poultice, washed and rebandaged my wound with the same care and sanitary precautions she used in changing a baby's diaper, saying as she did so, "Kind of Uncle George to bandage your bleeding finger. The tobacco has stopped the pain." Then, unfolding the handkerchief, she said, "And he has stained a perfectly good handkerchief. If I can get the yellow out when I wash it, I will send it home."

ISAAC ALLEN

In those beautiful days of June when lilac blossoms scented the air and songs of birds made melody, I loved the open air and mountain trails soft with soil. But the unbending pattern of behavior in my home was to go to church on Sundays. My mother never forced me to go to church, she persuaded—oh, how she persuaded. She had more approaches, reasons, arguments to guide my behavior than Satan has temptations. I went to church to please her. That Sunday in June I dragged my feet and looked at the ground the entire two blocks to the church house, ignoring the call of birds and aroma of lilacs.

In church I was aroused from my lethargic boredom by the fiery oratory of Isaac Allen. He had started his discourse on the "Second Coming of Christ" quietly, then, warming to the spirit, his voice grew big and bold, his delivery positive and powerful:

"Christ will come again in glory," he shouted.

I began to listen.

"He will come again," he repeated. "He will descend from heaven in a burst of heavenly light."

The intensity of his oratory was charging my spirit.

"The time of His coming is at hand," he shouted. "The righteous will behold the light, but its brightness will blind the eyes of the wicked. The righteous will hear His voice, but the ears of the wicked will be sealed. The righteous will rise like eagles to meet Him in the sky. Eye has not seen, nor ear heard, neither has entered the heart of man the glory, the happiness, the ecstasy of the righteous ones who are received at that hour in the arms of Jesus."

A flash of anger showed in the moist eyes of Isaac Allen as he continued, shouting in staccato rapidity.

"Be prepared with faith and good works! Cleanse yourselves from sin, for in that day the wicked will burn as stubble. They will creep into caves and hide behind rocks to escape from the presence of the Son of God."

Isaac Allen's sermon that day aroused my sensitivity; my heart was touched; he inflated my ten-year-old idealism; I went home contemplating the ways to wash away my sins.

Early the next morning my overwrought mind took me from bed and led me out to the back porch to look toward the east. Trees like tiny hairs on the distant mountaintop stood sentinel, screening the growing light where the sun would rise. Rapidly the rheostat, moved by the guiding hand of the universe, brought up the light. As I watched, it grew lighter and lighter, far brighter than the sun. When my eyes adjusted to the light, I saw plainly, standing tiptoe on the mountaintop, the Savior—in all His glory.

My mother came and joined me.

"Mama," I said, "the Savior has come! And, you see, I am not afraid, not hiding behind rocks. I see the light. Come, let's fly to meet Him!"

I heard a door slam. I opened my eyes, disoriented. I pushed the bed covers down and saw the darkness of the room pierced by a shaft of light from a slit at the side of the blind. "Why," I thought, "must I awake? Mother and I about to—it would have been great to fly—to fly to meet Him." I got up, went out the back door, and looked toward the east. The rising sun appeared to be resting in glory on the mountaintop.

Doc Woods

We knew him only as Doc, an appellation he had gained through selling salve, an ointment he concocted, purported to heal a multitude of bruises, wounds, and skin disorders. Doc was a big man, a bachelor who lived in a cabin hidden in aspen trees on the foothills in the Cedron area three miles west of town. Though old, he was tall and erect. His thick, untrimmed grey hair and beard, his loose coat and baggy trousers, his walking with a cane in firm strides in a winter storm, would remind one of the outcast King Lear.

He bore one more distinction: his nose, a unique nose, a nose that terminated in a pink, round ball with hills and hollows as if it had been molded by a waffle iron. His natural nose must have been pocked by smallpox. Doc's golf-ball proboscis was truly a nose of distinction.

Five or six of us boys were playing on the walk one recess when Doc came walking by. He had passed without any greetings when a boy called after him, "Hey, Doc, where did you get your nose?"

Doc stopped, turned, and walked back. The vocal boy and others ran away, apparently fearful of Doc and his cane. One other boy and I stayed. Doc spoke distinctly and emphatically. "Boys," he said, "what would you do if you had my nose?"

He turned and went on his way leaving us to think. How often since then have I been reminded that what can't be cured must, indeed, be endured.

Asa Hatch

Among the unfortunates in Victor was Asa Hatch, who suffered from a spasticity that disturbed his balance, making him walk like a drunken man—in fact, he was often taken for one. Sometimes a spasm would come and he would swing his head in a circling, nodding action that would almost make an observer dizzy. Neither his verbal nor his facial expression was totally free from distortion. Yet he communicated sensibly and often surprised people who did not know him with his wisdom and intelligence.

In summertime tourists often came in on the train en route to Jackson, Wyoming, the Teton Mountains, or Yellowstone Park. Victor people called these travelers "dudes" because some of them were en route to "dude ranches" for summer vacation.

One afternoon the C. M. Hatch General Merchandise Store overflowed with shoppers, Pete Hamblin and his whole family among them. The Hamblin children were not handsome. They were blessed with keen minds and cursed with ugly features. Children at school, in typical cruelty, called them Pete Hamblin's monkeys.

Also in the store that day were the Bresslers with their retarded son, big as a man, with the mind of a child—and looking mongoloid.

And Asa Hatch was there.

Then came in some "dudes." These tourists waited while the Hamblins and Bresslers finished shopping and left. As the tourists paid for their purchases, one said, "There are some peculiar people in this town."

The clerk smiled and paused. Asa Hatch, still there, being served by a clerk and standing by the tourist, heard the remark. He held his head still from a slight spasm and said slowly and distinctly, "Yes, there are, but when September comes, they all leave."

The Victim

A tragic story arose at the Victor cemetery, where my father was buried, that touched my tender heart. I must have been hardly old enough to enter school. The snow had gone and the ground was dry when we went to the cemetery at the base of the mountain, a mile east of town, to clean the graves. I wandered outside the graveyard fence, picking buttercups and johnny-jump-ups, where I found a mounded grave marked crudely with a native stone.

"Why," I asked my mother, "is that grave outside the cemetery?"

"It is the grave of a young woman who killed herself," she answered.

"Why did she?" I asked.

"Because her heart was broken."

"Why is she buried outside the graveyard?" I asked.

"It is a Christian cemetery," my mother explained, "and the church leaders wouldn't let them bury her in it."

"Why?" I asked.

Years went by, and the answers I got for that question never satisfied me. Later I realized that Mother hedged because she was caught between her loyalty to the church and her own convictions. The church had ruled that suicide was murder and that murderers could not share burial in the sacred ground reserved for saints.

Once I knew the name of the girl buried in the unworthy grave, and I knew her story.

She was young, narrowed down by regimentation to household duties and country chores. She had no better pleasures than to dress in her limited fineries, attend church, walk Sunday afternoons with the girls, attend an occasional dance or party, and engage in lively conversation with young people in gathering places.

In her day and her environment this girl's passionate nature found needs that were increased and developed by compliments and attention from men she met. Then she was irresistibly attracted to a man by feelings hitherto unknown. She saw nothing, heard nothing, felt nothing except in him. He was her all, her everything. Promises increased her hopes. With her intellect dulled, she reached the highest tension and surrendered to desire. Then—he left her.

She had no capacity to understand his action. Beside herself because he had betrayed her, she felt a uselessness, an abandonment, a silent sadness. And despite the attempts of others to console, she continued to feel the over-powering loneliness. Silently alone, she took her own life.

5

Reading, Writing, and Other Tricks, 1910–1917

TEACHER'S FALLEN ANGELS

Spelling class in Miss Grosch's fourth grade came in the sleepy hour of midafternoon when minutes dragged by like hours. In study time I would look lazily at each word and rehearse the letters in each silently. Then, when the words were dictated, I would be challenged by the inconsistencies of spelling. To be a good speller was desirable, I thought, but not of paramount importance. My ambition to learn to spell correctly was not aroused nor my application to study enforced; yet, I loved the sound of a report of 100 percent correct in spelling.

Miss Grosch's method of checking preparation was to dictate words to the class as we wrote them, have pupils exchange papers, then read the correct spelling while students checked each other's work, after which she called for reports, each student reporting the result for the pupil whose paper he had checked. The teacher used only two methods of exchanging papers: either with the student across the aisle, or with the one in front or behind. Thus, I always exchanged with June Dubois across the aisle or with Byron Curtis behind me.

Miss Grosch had called us her darlings, her little ladies and gentlemen, her little angels. Up to this time I had thought that she thought we were totally pure and undefiled. But now her undeviating methods of exchanging and correcting papers led two boys to accept the suggestion of the unseen monster of deceit. One said to the other, "You give me a hundred and I will give you a hundred." It worked. It worked so well that other children of the class, alert to the easy way to get grades of 100 percent, soon joined in the subterfuge. It became epidemic. Almost the whole class was corrupted.

When I exchanged with Byron behind me we both reported "a hundred," though both often misspelled words, but when I exchanged across the aisle it was different. June was incorruptible, having no need to cheat since she always spelled correctly. When the teacher called the name "June," I would report truthfully, "a hundred"; when the teacher called "Thomas," June would report, correctly, "one wrong," or whatever the result.

One day, however, when I had exchanged with June and she had reported "one wrong" for me while everyone else in the class had received "a hundred," the teacher called for all papers to be handed in, for she had heard or perceived the presence of evil in the classroom. She checked all the papers herself and found proof of astonishing corruption. We had become fallen angels. This inspired her to present a lesson on honesty.

"You have all been bad boys and girls," she began. "All except two. You have cheated and told falsehoods. Only two of you are upright and truthful, June and Thomas. Will you two stand and be honored? The rest of you should hang your heads in shame."

I stood with June. I did not want to stand.

The Other Cheek

Among the virtues that my mother taught me as a child was that of pacifism. "Do not fight," she said. "Cowards fight. Only cowards strike others weaker than themselves."

I had a problem. My mother always spoke well of my deceased father. He was kind, a loving husband, a hard worker, a bright light in my mother's eyes, "but"—there was a "but"—"but he let others take advantage of him, he would not *fight* for his rights." Those were her words. The picture that she and others gave me of my father led me to believe that at bargaining he was a failure, at horse trading a disaster. His worry was that he might lose money for the other fellow. In the pioneer country of the Tetons where commerce existed chiefly by barter, my father could have been voted the best barter bait. One problem I faced was this: with a father like that and a mother who said, "Give to him that asks of you! Turn the other cheek! Do not fight!" how could I be anything but milk toast?

There were other inconsistencies. Mother talked as if my father should have had the fighting spirit. She broke the passive rule herself by switching me when I needed it. My teacher whipped Calvin Shirtz with a paddle when he dipped the ends of the long blond hair of the girl in front of him in his inkwell. Boys bloodied each other's noses on the schoolground. It was a fighting world.

One day my fourth-grade teacher called, "Take your seats." I took my seat but left my foot in the aisle. A big awkward boy, Tim Johnson, lumbered down the aisle and stumbled over my foot. He got up off the floor, rubbing the lip cut by his teeth when he fell on his chin. He turned and was ready to strike me, but Miss Grosch's eagle eye forced a retreat.

That brought a challenge—a note from my newly acquired enemy, stealthily slipped to me during school, reading, "I'll meet you behind the grandstand after school." Every kid knew that "behind the grandstand" meant "fight." That was the place where victors and vanquished, heroes and cowards were made. Only the basest of cowards would refuse to meet a challenger behind the grandstand. I had to go there even though I knew that win or lose I would get a whipping when I got home.

Behind the grandstand older boys made rules to keep fighting fair. Spectators came to cheer or chide one or the other of the contestants. I went into the ring, trembling with fright, hanging my head in shame. Big Tim Johnson stood there stern and stoic.

"What are we fighting for?" I asked.

"You tripped me," he said.

"Not on purpose," I said.

"On purpose," he said.

"I did not."

"You did too."

"Put a chip on his shoulder," a voice said.

"Knock it off now, Tommy," the voice said.

"Why?" I said.

"Rules," the voice called.

I pushed it off. Then, wow! Before I could move, Tim struck me a blow in the face. This made me mad, so I ran to him and slapped his face in fast blows—bang, bang, bang. Spectators laughed. The referee yelled, "Stop! Ye can't slap. Ye gotta hit with yer fists." Then after a pause he called, "Go."

Before I made a move I received a blow on the chin that sent me sprawling. Angry now, I jumped up vowing revenge, and before he could clench a fist I kicked him my strongest kick on the shin and with my hands pulled his hair.

"Stop," yelled the referee, "Ye can't kick and ye can't pull hair."

"Why?" I asked.

"Rules."

At that juncture I knew that I had lost the fight, for they had ruled out all the methods of fighting my sisters had taught me.

A half hour later I arrived home in defeat with bloody mouth and nose, torn shirt, and subdued spirits to meet Mother. She met me with sympathy. Her concerns seemed to be, in order, me, my bloody face, my torn and soiled clothes, and my getting into a fight.

The next day at school I met my strongest rooter at the fight, cousin Eugene, three years older than I. He said, "You could a licked Tim if you'd a known how to fight. If you want to learn I'll teach you."

For weeks after that I often went over to Eugene's to play. But we did not play; he taught me to fight, both defense and offense. He taught me how to keep moving to hold my balance, how to dodge blows, how to protect my face with my hands, how to move fast and take advantage of my opponent's pauses, how to put my weight behind a stiff arm blow, and how to take blows, some of which he freely gave me to toughen me up. In short, he taught me everything about fighting.

Then at school I slipped a note to Tim Johnson: "Meet me after school behind the grandstand."

Tim came to the fight with the confidence of having had an easy win in the previous encounter. I went with the secret of my new power.

"What are we fighting for?" he asked.

"To get even," I said.

The referee inspected our hands to see that neither of us had brass knucks, then said, "Go."

I immediately saw the opportunity to pull a trick I had learned. I moved fast, lowered my head, braced myself, and before he was ready struck my most powerful blow squarely in his belly. He bent forward, gasped, and lost his composure. Then I gave him an uppercut in the face, staggering him. He regained poise and struck at my nose with all his power. I had learned to dodge. With my long neck I could have out-dodged "Alfalfa," the skinny, cross-eyed kid in the "Our Gang" movies. I had learned to move my head out of the path of the fastest fist. I dodged Tim's blow so completely that he lost his balance and fell down, hurting himself. The crowd of spectators roared with laughter. The referee called time out while my opponent got up.

At the signal to begin again Tim came at me with mad-dog rage, for he seethed with anger and suffered with shame at his own awkward fall. He struck at me again and again, but he could not find my face. I was so busy dodging that I could not strike a blow. I just let him strike and miss until he tuckered out. Then I struck, caught his nose with my second blow and his chin with the third, and he fell with a bloody nose. The referee ran over and lifted my hand high in the air.

I heard noise from the crowd. As they quieted down the referee said, "I want you two to shake hands."

I reached out my hand. Tim morosely put his limp hand in mine. "We're even," I said.

He didn't answer.

When I Stopped Smoking

Mrs. Cluff taught school. She molded the minds of fifth-graders in the impressive two-story white limestone schoolhouse with the high front bell tower housing the bell, the loud call of which pulled children to it like a dinner bell. On a certain day my determination never to smoke a cigarette again might not have occurred had the ding-dong of the bell reached my ear a minute sooner. Indeed, my repentance might never have emerged without the schoolhouse, the bell, and my teacher, Mrs. Cluff.

Mrs. Cluff was an experienced molder of minds, and my mind was putty in her hands, evidence of which will presently be obvious.

In those days before Kaiser Wilhelm and Adolf Hitler had turned America sour on goose-step, we marched in military precision in and out of school. At dismissal time the buzzer would sound. The teacher would call for attention. Then, as she called "one," we would sit erect; at "two," turn; at "three," stand; at "four," turn ready to march. When the piano rang out from the hall in stirring march time, the teacher would call, "Left right, left right, forward march," and we marched in one row out the door where we fell into line two abreast, and finally four abreast at the top of the stairs, to march down and outside where, after halting and after careful alignment, we were released by order of the principal.

One afternoon recess period a pupil, Ed Robertson, chanced to fall in line with me as we marched and whispered to me (against rules), "I got a sack of Bull Durham." A fifth-grade boy with a sack of tobacco! Wow! My curiosity was aroused at the courage of a boy to carry a sack of tobacco; I shadowed him on the school ground. He gathered two friends and the four of us hunted for a hiding place and found it in the nearby church house, which had been conveniently left unlocked. There Ed Robertson produced the tobacco, cigarette papers, and matches, and then proceeded to roll his own. He handed the makings to the next boy, who did likewise. At last my turn came. I found that rolling a cigarette was a skill I had not acquired through casual observance of men making them. I did not fold the paper right, I did not roll it tight over the tobacco, and my licking the paper failed to stick it fast. However, after repeated trials I had something loosely like a cigarette—loosely indeed. With a match I tried to find fire in the seat of my overalls as men did. The clanging of the school bell struck my ears as my match struck fire. Determined not to make my creation a complete loss, I quickly put the match to the cigarette and took a draw. Then, coughing, I threw the cigarette away and with the other boys ran for school.

In the schoolroom Mrs. Cluff's alert sensory perception was not deceived. She smelled something that brought the comment, "Someone in this room has been smoking, and I intend to find out who." Then she started at the far side of the room to ask every boy, "Did you smoke?" Ed Robertson was the first of the guilty to be asked. "Yes, Ma'am," he answered, as if he were saying, "Today I became a man."

As the teacher's inquiry continued, I was thinking. I thought that surely one puff on a loppy cigarette could not be called smoking. Yet, I had rolled it, lit it, and puffed on it. In the meantime Mrs. Cluff's inquisition reached Marion Thompson and Dane Larson, who each confessed. I heard other innocent boys say, "No," "No," "No," as the questioning approached me. Mrs. Cluff's piercing eye caught mine as she asked, "Did you smoke?" In that moment I decided. I made the decision. I answered, "No, Ma'am."

Immediately three voices chorused, "He did too."

I was overwhelmed and totally inarticulate, convicted by a jury of my peers. But Mrs. Cluff became eloquent. She lectured on and on, continuous as a dripping faucet. "Smoking," she said, "stunts the user physically." As she talked, I saw myself a pony beside a work horse, then a Bantam rooster beside a Dominique; I became the stunted pig, the Tom Thumb. The tobacco furnace was shrinking my already miniature frame.

"It stunts the user's mentality," she continued. Now, as I envisioned the tobacco bite into my mentality, my remorse became overwhelming. Tomorrow I would be duller than today. My already atrocious spelling could not take it.

"The use of tobacco stunts the smoker morally," she continued. And on this moral devastation she used the ready example. She looked my way. "Here is a boy," she said, as she pointed an accusing finger at me, "here is a boy who usually is honest. Today he smoked. Already he is telling lies." I squirmed in my seat. I shrank in my desk. My degeneracy engulfed me. I became a worm. My salvation was in jeopardy. Just before the buzzer sounded to release school for the day, Mrs. Cluff said, "Now, if you naughty boys will go right home and tell your mothers that you smoked, you may partially redeem yourselves."

I could hardly wait to get home. I had to prove that tobacco had not annihilated my morals. I ran the entire two blocks to my home, saying to myself, "The devil hasn't got me yet." I ran up to Mother, looked up into her face, and said, "Mama, I smoked."

"You what?" she said.

"I smoked."

"You smoked. Mercy, who with?"

"Ed Robertson, Dane Larson, and Marion Thompson."

"Naughty boys! Well . . . ," she said, "well, when did you smoke?"

"Afternoon recess."

"Where in the world could you smoke at recess?"

"In the church house."

"In the church house? Defile the House of the Lord? Good gracious, you might have burned it down."

This was another sin I had committed unawares. Mother went on saying things about being reverent.

The interrogation went on to extract from me the first and last detail of the recess adventure into sin. Finally she said, "You say that if the bell had rung a minute sooner, you never would have got it lit. But you intended to smoke, so you are guilty. The thing to do now is never to intend to smoke."

When the conference was over, I went outside. It was getting dark now. I looked toward the church house and observed that it was still standing. That day I stopped smoking.

CLARENCE STEPHENS

Once a year, along with Thanksgiving feasting, Christmas cheer, and Fourth of July elation came a lesser heralded excitement to our town: the coming of teachers for the new school year. In those days, new residents in town were a rarity. This year, among the lovely young ladies who arrived and sparked the courtship game of older boys, came my eighth-grade teacher, Mr. Stephens, a handsome young man with a wife and two children. The first month of school I feared him, the second month I cheered him.

That year I hated Leo Wardle, a classmate; a retention and therefore a bigger, older, stronger boy. He teased me by yelling, "Tommy, Tommy titmouse / Laid an egg in our house / Egg was rotten good for nothing / So was Tommy titmouse." He wrestled my marbles away from me and never returned them. He sat behind me and poked me in the back. Like a botfly in a horse's nose he stung me. I declared I hated him, which amplified my hate. When he spurred me in the back one day and whispered, "Loan me some paper," I searched my vocabulary for the meanest words I could write to repulse him. On a sheet of my tablet I wrote in big, underlined, illuminated words, "Kiss My Ass!" and held it up for him to see.

Later, when I had forgotten Leo and likewise had forgotten my anger and my art and had left it on display, Mr. Stephens walked down the aisle and saw it. He looked at me long and saw my shrinking self-esteem. "If that came out of your mind," he said, pointing at it, "leave it out, and if you think it is art, show it to your mother and get her opinion."

A PEARL-HANDLED POCKETKNIFE

In my thirteenth year the most inspiring book I knew was the Sears-Roebuck Catalog—my wish book. In it I possessed all the things I saw and could not buy. I wanted new clothes, a watch, a saddle for our horse, a bicycle—hundreds of things from phonographs to pocketknives. Oh, how I wanted a pearl-handled, three-blade pocketknife. I turned often to the page in the catalog to feast my eyes on the picture of the coveted pocketknife. But I could not buy it. I did not have the money. I could not earn the money, and my mother could not raise the money. That I knew.

At this time, when my desire for a pocketknife overshadowed all other desires, the local C. M. Hatch General Merchandise Store in our town displayed an array of pocketknives, among them a pearl-handled, three-blade beauty marked $1.75. At every opportunity I went the two blocks from my home to the store to ogle and admire the knife. Then one day I found myself alone in the sales area of the store, the two clerks in the back room unpacking merchandise. I took the bright-shining knife out of the display, fondled it in my hands, opened and closed the blades, and put it in my pocket to test and enjoy the feel of it. Then with sudden decision I went out of the store possessor of the knife. Outside I ran a block toward home, stopped, took the knife out, opened the blades, and for some time in my happiness let the world go by.

Then I began to think how I must hide my precious possession from my sisters, who would question me or tell my mother that I had it. I could not leave it in my pocket at night, for Mother might find it. If I took the knife to school, the boys would ask, "Where did you get that knife?" I would answer, "I bought it." And they would say, "You did not, because you could not raise that kind of money." The more I thought about my theft, the more trouble I could see. Dejected, I returned to the store, loitered around until the clerks were busy elsewhere and customers were not watching. Then I stealthily returned the knife to the display.

In school that year my teacher, Mr. Stephens, promoted a homework project. He provided us with report sheets each week on which we were asked to report hours spent at home on schoolwork, housework, various chores, and special projects. For special projects he encouraged us to make things, original things that could be exhibited, put on display for parents and patrons to see. He announced that winners in this homework project would be honored, a thing in which I took little interest. But for the fun of it I got my mother to allow me to use my deceased father's good carpenter tools to build a bedside stand. I worked hard on this, planing the boards, sanding them, cutting and fitting, and finally finishing the stand with many coats of varnish. I also wove on Mother's loom a decorative rug, 26 inches by 52 inches.

In making reports I was careless. Some weeks I failed to hand in my work-hour sheets until prodded by the teacher. I worked not for honor, but for my mother who had convinced me that we all had to work to survive. I fed and milked cows. I sawed and chopped wood and did other chores aside from working on my projects, all of which put hours on the reports.

For exhibit day I took my rug and table to school, rather proud of my creations, yet not possessed with the competitive spirit. The next day in the exhibit room I was utterly surprised to find a blue ribbon on my rug reading, "First Prize." In all that array of pillows, sewing, needlework, scrapbooks, art, and various woodwork creations of aspiring carpenters, my rug had won first prize. I couldn't believe it.

That afternoon when parents and teachers were assembled in the project exhibit room for the party, the principal presented many awards. Then at last he presented to me the Grand Prize for Homework and Project—a three-blade, pearl-handled pocketknife presented by the C. M. Hatch General Merchandise Store.

GIFFORD, THE MUSIC MAN

The town council had an ambitious dream, to have a band—ambitious indeed for a scattered populace of six or seven hundred rural residents.

"We have talent in our community," the chairman of the board, C. M. Hatch, argued. "Music is sustenance for the soul. Band music matches our mountains. We need and should have a town band."

Undoubtedly the fact that Driggs, the neighboring community, had pleasantly surprised the valley residents with a band that led the last Independence Day parade sparked the Victor town council into competitive action.

With village funds they bought several band instruments. Then they hired Irvin Robertson, a young man who had been away to college and knew music, to build a band. He rounded up a few tooters to toot and be tutored and brought out of the closets every band instrument that had found resting place in that end of the valley. Robertson played a trumpet. One or two others who joined the band had instruments and could read and play simple music. I applied for admission and received custody of a new, city-owned alto horn. Most of us aspiring horn blowers brought in from the woods and the farms knew the rhythm of a woodpecker pounding on a tree, the song of the meadowlark, the bugling of the male elk in mating season—all the sounds of nature. The music of nature, however, is a mountain and a valley away from book music of bars, scales, eighth, quarter, half, and full notes, sharps, flats, forte, pianissimo, and all the rest.

At the first gathering I received my horn. I put the mouthpiece to my mouth, as did other novices, tightened my lips, and blew into it. The sounds that came from horns that night might have made a deaf man pleased with his limitation. We possessed as much coordination as a gathering of mongrel dogs. The overwhelming ignorance of music that many of us showed must have left the director in despair. But Irvin Robertson knew music and persisted. He found, however, that some of these aspiring musicians had no ear and some no rhythm. Some had no mind to learn a scale and some no interest after they found they could not play "music" after the first lesson. Membership dwindled. After a few months, twenty diminished to ten. The band failed even to be able to play "My Country, 'Tis of Thee" for the Fourth of July celebration.

Then Lamont Gifford came to town, after invitation of the school board, to teach music in the schools. Gifford was a young married man of twenty obsessed with enormous drive for music. He was the original Norman Vincent Peale, philosopher of positive thinking, the eternal optimist. He possessed the energy of a young puppy. What he lacked in musical knowledge or skill, he made up for with limitless self-confidence and a contagious enthusiasm that he communicated to his students. In the community there were those who thought that he loved himself with such amplitude and tenderness and charity that no love would be left for his students. They were wrong. He loved the young people and led them with a certain charisma. He made every pupil feel important. One slide pusher under his leadership could feel as powerful as seventy-six trombones. He had unheard-of capacity to interest everybody in music.

The city-owned instruments were given to the school, and school-age survivors of the Robertson band became the inheritance of the new music man. I bought a trumpet and gave up the alto horn. To Gifford I was a budding genius. He could tolerate my blasts and discords while working for harmony. He could whip his pupils into line, work them unmercifully, and at the same time make music a delightful game. By the end of the first school year Gifford took the thirty-piece band to Idaho Falls and gave a concert. Nearly one-half of all the students of Victor High School played in the band. That Fourth of July Mr. Gifford's band made the American flag flutter with patriotic reverberations of "The Star Spangled Banner." Residents swelled with pride to hear the mountains alive with music. If the drummer missed a beat or a trumpet or two failed to reach the high notes of "the rocket's red glare," no one seemed to care, for Victor had a band that outnumbered, outshone, and outblasted the Driggs band.

6

High School Daze, 1918

RED HAIR IN THE SACRED GROVE

In my library is a small book, a 1912 Macmillan edition of *Othello, the Moor of Venice*, with the name of Katheryn Spurns on the fly-leaf. On the title page the name appears again with part of an address, 236 Mourning, and no city or state. I possess it—it is with me, a chronic chastisement to my sensitivity. It stands among Shakespeare's works an ever-present apologue, a potent irony on "He who steals my purse steals trash."

The owner of the book was my teacher when I was in the eleventh grade, the year of the Armistice. She came into my Idaho town on the train just before school started. I remember the town as it looked then. Anyone getting off the train could see most of it at a glance: the front of the brick hotel, the church tower, the sandstone schoolhouse from the back, and, in the distance, the messy backyards of the two stores, a livery barn, a warehouse, and various dwellings.

A broken cement- and boardwalk led from the depot to the hotel passing an ugly, unpainted storehouse with a pigpen behind. Rocks lay on several vacant lots like large potatoes, intermixed here and there with spears of brown and shriveled grass.

In those days I often ran from home two blocks away to meet the one daily train when it pulled into the depot. I remember the day Miss Spurns arrived. A section hand was standing there by the train leaning on his bar (the train coming in had temporarily put him out of work), gazing unabashedly at the four or five people getting off the train. Straight in front of the passenger car of the mixed train stood several people: a woman with scraggly hair and a sunbonnet, a freckled boy with a broken suspender, and an old man with watery eyes leaning on a cane. The drayman driving a mangy-looking team of unmatched horses hitched to an old wide-tired Bain wagon had just said "Whoa" to his team at the mail car door a few steps ahead of the passenger car exit, and the station agent had come out of his office to say something to the drayman. The horses breathed pungent air down the neck of another bystander, Nephi Boseman, a high school senior from the West Side. Water leaked in little streams from the water tank beside the track, making little puddles in which two children had been playing, but now with the train coming to a halt they stood polka-dotted with mud, one holding a stick and the other a can, peering at the people. And I was there by the corner of the depot in my old knickers. Miss Spurns emerged from the car with a dude passenger. She glanced around momentarily, while her red hair moved in the autumn air and her brown coat shone glossy in the sun, and said emphatically to her escort, "My God, what a dump."

She spoke plainly, ignoring the country eyes upon her that now peered more penetratingly through what the ears heard. All bystanders reacted. Even the deaf drayman thought he heard, and punctuated the comment with a swish of tobacco juice.

When high school started, all seventy pupils knew what Miss Spurns had said. They would not tolerate a teacher who hated their town and their parents could not tolerate a teacher who swore.

To some people Miss Spurns became at once the Ichabod Crane of the community. Indeed, she had a great deal in common with him: long legs projecting somewhat too far below her skirts, long arms protruding too far beyond her leather coat, and big bony hands hanging incongruously around. She became a common sight in the village, her red hair, not wholly untidy, flying in the wind as she walked with big steps, her torso listing to the front from her hips upward, and her leather coat, long enough to reach halfway from her hips to her knees, refusing to make the turn with the contour of her body at the waist and continuing the angle behind like the eaves of a smoke-house.

In the classroom Miss Spurns permitted no clowning. A dedicated teacher, she planned her work, prepared her assignments, drilled and tested her students, and checked their papers meticulously. I remember how the first day in Junior English class she assigned a theme of five hundred words and other heavy reading assignments for the first week that brought complaints which grew intensely as the week wore by and pupils learned that the reading was from a writer, Chaucer, who wrote in a well-nigh incomprehensible language.

When a few weeks of school had passed, the principal had listened to complaints from the students about assignments, and from parents, too, who joined with their children in righteous indignation at such a travesty of justice.

At this time when tender minds were being unmercifully stretched, some students found things in Chaucer not fit for consumption. Miss Spurns, in reading the conclusion of "The Pardoner's Tale," read the line, "Thogh it were with thy fundement depeint," which she failed to interpret or explain.

"What does that mean?" asked Nephi.

"To translate word for word," said Miss Spurns, "it means, 'Though it were with thy excrement stained.' "

"What does 'excrement' mean?" asked Nephi.

"Manure," answered the teacher.

Nephi and other pupils laughed.

"Students," shouted Miss Spurns sternly, "grow up." She was angry. "You people are so self-righteous in this community that you pretend to be shocked by your own language. Chaucer could have used another word instead of 'fundement,' a word you know because it is not as cultured. In 'The Miller's Tale' he uses words that are crude to show how vulgar the Miller was, the same words you and your brothers and your fathers use. You would scoff at them in Chaucer because you cannot understand the artistic purpose. If you know Shakespeare at all, you think he is a lesser writer than Harold Bell Wright. You think your Eliza Snow is a greater musician than Handel. You probably have never heard of Rembrandt, but if you had you would think that that sloppy painting of *The Sacred Grove* above the pulpit in your chapel is greater than his *Christ Healing the Sick*. You have no aesthetic sense, no concept of beauty. You people in this class will not allow yourselves to like Chaucer—my God, what poverty."

I was angry at Miss Spurns. I was beginning to get the pleasant sound of Chaucer's language, to enjoy his humor, his pathos, his freedom of expression, and now I was falsely accused. Yet there was something in Miss Spurns's wrathful indignation that pleased me.

Sitting on the steps of the limestone meetinghouse (which was also used for school) that noontime, eating sandwiches and enjoying the western sun of the early winter day, Ralph fingered his anthology and found in "The Miller's Tale" the forbidden words referred to by the teacher. He laughed as he handed the book to me.

"Can it really mean what it says?" I asked as we peered at the page. I had never seen such words in print except on untidy walls of public outhouses around town. I read again and knew I read right. We laughed. Nephi, sitting below, looking and smelling like a cowboy, said, "Read it to me; I can't read the damn stuff."

Ralph read a few lines aloud. At that moment June Dubois came around the corner with Erma Jones. Ralph quite successfully camouflaged the cause of the merriment as I did until Nephi, not habitually concerned with the truth, now earnestly made sure to let it wholly out. He grabbed the open book. "Read it," he said, handing it to Erma.

Erma saw it was Chaucer and handed it to June, a modest little girl who rarely smiled, who had spent far more time with books than with boys, and who was slow-witted enough not to suspect the trickery of her classmate.

Erma, less book-learned though a better observer, stopped June before she began to read aloud, and the two girls' noses met above the book.

In a moment June dropped her hands, turned purple in the face, glanced menacingly at Nephi, and broke away from Erma to dash across the street toward the drugstore.

Miss Spurns's circle of interested observers in school and out grew in number and intensity. Since many of the six hundred people of the school district knew Miss Spurns only by hearsay, her personality developed in various directions. Nephi Boseman called her the Wife of Bath, a character he knew only through her teaching. The pool-hall loafers called her "the broad." A group of Relief Society ladies called her worldly. A more kindly group said she was a person capable of being good, but one who needed a good man to keep her in line.

Monday class time the teacher specified as theme day. On that day she would comment on themes and return them to students. She began one day talking to the class about a set of themes she had read: "Ralph's theme is accurate in sentence structure, fair in punctuation—even *good* I should say for high-school work—and in content fair, though somewhat purposeless. Nephi's theme as usual is a pleasure to me, a pleasure because I always wonder what it might contain. Occasionally when I find a word I can identify I am overjoyed." Her voice showed her amused irony. "Talitha, your mechanics are bad, though an improvement is observable over your first theme; in fact, this paper might be acceptable if you had anything to say. Do write about something significant. Virginia, as before, you have done an excellent piece of writing as regards construction, organization, and clarity. The quarrel I have with you is with your subject matter. Your argument is unsound; it lacks logic. Your title, 'The True Church,' is a satisfactory statement of the content. In the body you say that Joseph Smith saw God and Jesus and that Jesus told Joseph Smith that all the churches were an abomination to God. Then you say that God had Joseph Smith organize the true church and that all other churches are wrong. Virginia, is that what you said?"

"Yes," Virginia said, quite weakly. "That is what *we believe.*"

"You believe that all the churches except yours are an abomination before God?" the teacher asked increduously.

Virginia nodded.

"Do you believe, then, that only your church people are in favor with God?"

"They are the only ones who will get to the celestial glory," Virginia explained.

"Then you are telling me that I, a Methodist, will not get to heaven."

"I did not mean to, Miss Spurns."

Virginia now was nearly in tears. Feeling that someone should help her, I volunteered. "Miss Spurns, you could join the church, or, if you don't, the work can be done for you after you are dead."

"What do you mean, work done for me after I am dead?"

"I mean . . . well . . . someone can be baptized for you."

Miss Spurns laughed, then said with a smile, "No, you can't. I won't let you be baptized for me."

The class laughed, and she continued. "No, students, you think about your religion. My people are good people; my minister is a good man—and you say only Mormons will go to heaven. Is that logic?"

"Do your people all swear?" interrupted Nephi.

Miss Spurns flashed anger in darkening eyes. "Perhaps we do, Nephi, but we do not say *ain't* and *comin'* and *goin'* and *I seen it* and *I clumb it*—don't you ever swear, Nephi, tell me, don't you swear?"

"Yes, I do," said Nephi boastingly, "but I ain't goin' to heaven."

"No, and you are not going to get credit for this class unless you correct your language."

"Yes," continued Miss Spurns, nodding to Virginia, whose hand was raised.

"You could go the terrestrial degree of glory without joining the church," Virginia said.

"Terrestrial," said Miss Spurns, thinking. "Terrestrial comes from the French *terra* meaning 'earth.' What do you mean, terrestrial glory?"

"It is a heaven a little lower than the celestial," explained Virginia. "Only the people who are baptized can go to the celestial glory."

To the whole group, the teacher now spoke more softly: "What poor, innocent lambs you are. You know so little about this life, and you are ready to go to the highest heaven. You think that you could take a moron out and baptize him, and though he is filthy as a dung hill, inane as a clod, or lazy as a sparrow, he has a ticket to heaven."

Class was dismissed and all themes had been handed back except mine. I went to the teacher's desk.

"Yours was not worth commenting on or reading," she told me. "It showed disrespect for teachers, and you and this community need to be taught something about culture and manners."

I turned and walked away. Never before had I been accused by a teacher of being disrespectful. The theme was humorous, I thought, but she did not see it.

Miss Spurns loved Shakespeare, the writer who stood boldly above all other writers, the man with the great invisible power, the supreme articulate, the wisest, the wittiest, the most inspired and inspiring writer of all time—all this Miss Spurns taught. And she read the plays with such poetic expression and meaning that I, too, learned to like Shakespeare. Under her forceful drive, Shakespeare rose out of the past to become a great citizen of the world I lived in. I watched the teacher and saw the sparkle in her hard eyes as she read something she loved. I saw her become Shylock demanding his pound of flesh and Portia pleading for mercy. Shakespearean images under her tongue became visions. The forests in which I had wandered became the magical forest of Arden with books in its running brooks, and the continuous wintry winds I thought of now as "counsellors that feelingly persuaded him who he is." English class to me became a pleasure to anticipate, and reading the assignments a delightful discipline. Miss Spurns read Lady Macbeth's speech:

> I have given suck and know
> How tender 'tis to love the babe that milks me.
> I would while it was yet smiling in my face
> Have plucked the nipple from his boneless gums,
> And dashed his brains out, had I sworn, as you
> Have done to this.

Then I saw the hardness in the teacher's face, which I had seen before when she scornfully denounced the earthy people of the community. I heard classmates say, "She would, she would kill her own baby."

I also heard her read speeches of the humbled Lady Macbeth, washing her hands and crying, "Here is the smell of blood still," and the doctor's speech, "What a sigh is there! The heart is sorely charged." But in this I saw another Miss Spurns.

Students, angered at the teacher's repeated charges of shallow provincialism in the community and her incessant demands for letter-perfect work, were griping unmercifully. But I was not aware of the extremes to which townspeople had caught fire with the generated heat of wagging tongues until another event occurred.

The man who had the greatest influence and say in the community was C. M. Hatch, chairman of the school board, owner of the C. M. Hatch and Company General Merchandise Store. I felt honored when Mr. Hatch called me behind the swinging gate of his office in the back of his store just beyond the potbellied stove.

Mr. Hatch was impressive with his grey hair crowning his pale, unwrinkled face, his spotlessly clean clothes, and his easy flow of language. "About this Miss Spurns," he asked, "how do you think she is succeeding as a teacher?"

"Do you mean . . . just what do you mean? With all the students?"

"Are you learning, becoming educated, under her tutelage?"

"Yes, Mr. Hatch," I said, quite inarticulately.

"What do you students think of her ability to lead you to learn and understand literature and to use better language in speaking and writing?"

I hesitated.

"Your reluctance to talk about your teacher, son, is quite justifiable, but we have a problem. You know, many people are complaining. In our town is a faction we could call the I-have-the-Lord people. Now with Miss Spurns these people are causing trouble. They are the people who think they are magnifying their priesthood when they are magnifying other people's sins. These people know they belong to God's Kingdom, are among the elect, the chosen of the chosen. Actually they have narrowed God to an infinitesimal smallness, to a few specifics they understand themselves, and they see no purpose in many of the educational values possessed by Miss Spurns."

I was agreeing with Mr. Hatch.

"These I've-got-the-Lord zealots, though relatively few, are winning many people of the other groups to their cause; right now, many people are agitating the school board toward revocation of Miss Spurns's contract. That is why I am asking you questions; I've got to get the facts with which to judge this teacher."

I hoped I could honestly report.

"Specifically," Mr. Hatch went on, "they claim Miss Spurns attacks the church, teaches false doctrine, swears, exposes the pupils to vulgarity, is herself immodest, considers herself better than we, and is guilty of carrying on flirtatious affairs with men from over the hill. Are these charges in your opinion made in all justice? Does she swear in school?"

"Yes, she has."

"Has she attacked principles of our religion?"

"Yes, sir," I said; I wished that I had words to explain.

"Do you know of a time when she raised her skirts and exposed her body to the students?"

"I was at a school party when she ran against a bench and fell—we were playing fill-the-gap—and she raised her dress to show how she had skinned her knee."

Mr. Hatch smiled. "That wound has moved upward since the accident," he said, then continued with his questions.

"Has she assigned you stories to read which contained vile language, and do you personally know of any indecent behavior of this young lady in her associations with men from Jackson Hole?"

"I have seen her with men, sir . . . a man from Jackson . . ."

"A Boseman boy from the West Side," broke in the chairman, "is responsible for circulation of some scandalous details of her private life. Do you know of this—of the reliability of this information?"

"The boys can see through her window from the top of the warehouse behind the hotel," I said.

"Even a schoolteacher would hardly expect a warehouse to have eyes on its roof," Mr. Hatch said with a sardonic smile.

I left the chairman's office in melancholy, sorry for my inability to put everything in its context, to show how Miss Spurns had something from the big world of literature and life that people of the town did not have, and how she had opened up that world for us to see.

Back at school, I resolved to uphold the teacher at all costs, for I chafed under the sting of conscience for having failed to do so before the chairman of the board.

Early one day before school began, I went toward the little room used by the church for a kitchen and by Miss Spurns for a combined classroom and office. As I approached through the bigger room I could see the desk, through the open door, unoccupied, though overwhelmed with books and papers. Then as I came nearer I saw Miss Spurns leaning to the floor, her back to me, trying to replace the broken draft door on the coal range that furnished heat for the room. For speedy heating the janitor had left the door off. Now, with the room warm, the stove red with heat, Miss Spurns was attempting to cut off the draft. I was too disturbed in my thought to give more than a glance to the womanly figure, dressed this morning in her lovely white knit dress and silk stockings. I stood thinking, feeling misplaced, afraid to speak while her hips waved before me in a way hardly compatible with her dignity. I feared that this inconvenience of trying again to get this broken door to hang in place would bring a tirade against the destructive heathen of the high school or the dilatory school board who failed to have it repaired.

Then, having met with success, Miss Spurns stood, turned to come to her desk, and saw me. Almost without emotion she said, "You will note, Thomas, that I replaced the exasperating thing without vocal invective."

I smiled without speaking.

She looked at me as though she expected something from me. But I was slow; before superiors, words deserted me. Hesitantly I moved toward the desk at which she had arrived and managed to say, "Miss Spurns, you are leaving Shakespeare in English." Immediately I knew I had not said what I wanted to say and that I had said it awkwardly. "What I mean is, I am sorry . . . I hoped . . . I hoped you would teach *Othello*. You rec—rec—commended it, you know."

The teacher did not speak. I felt as if I were in a spelling match and it was my turn to spell a word, a word I did not know.

I continued, "I like—"

"I know you do. I know you like Shakespeare," Miss Spurns added with a smile. "I have been discouraged with my work here, but I am beginning to feel success. Now that I see some sparks of interest in some of you, I will not be as impatient, cross, and impetuous."

"You have had reason," I said.

"This is my first year out of college, Thomas, and I think now that I have expected too much. I have expected of you what my teachers in college demanded of me."

I could think of nothing to say.

"I remember, Thomas, that some weeks ago I mistreated you, called you discourteous. I want to apologize, because I was wrong."

"Thank you, Miss Spurns."

"You were asking about studying *Othello*," she continued. "You could read it yourself, you know; I could loan you the book."

"Oh, no, I might lose it, or have an accident, or fail to return it."

"You will protect it and return it; I am not afraid to loan it to you," she said.

I left the teacher's room content with the accepted apology and the proffered book; yet I felt an oppressive awareness of my failure to tell Miss Spurns what I wanted her to know.

On the following Friday, school had been called and teachers were attempting to generate in pupils some intellectual yearning when a message from the school board demanded an immediate recess for a joint meeting of the board and the three-member faculty. The principal announced that classes would be reconvened before noon and all students should respond at bell call.

Pandemonium immediately broke loose. I heard a voice from behind say, "They are going to can Spurns." Someone near said, "No more good window peeping for Nephi."

The principal was coming toward me. Instinctively I thought of this man as a loaded gun, loaded now with ammunition for me and undoubtedly loaded to avenge some wrong done or duty undone. "Thomas," the principal was saying, "the board has asked me to bring you to the meeting."

Though frightened at the thought, I knew no recourse but to obey.

At the beginning of the board meeting, while cordiality edged its way around, I looked from one to another of the group—no one dressed for the occasion, each betraying his own occupation: Mr. Davis in carpenter's white overalls and shiny black shoes; Mr. Hatch in his white shirt and black half-sleeves to the elbow, dress pants, and vest with gold watch chain across it; Mr. Brussels in faded blue denim overalls and jumper and high-topped overshoes discolored a barnyard yellow.

Miss Spurns sat with her auburn hair glistening brightly, her eyes alert; I recalled how in class she had smelled like perfumed soap. I looked again at Mr. Brussels. High on the leg of his overalls was a dirty spot, round like the top of a can and stringing funnel-like at the bottom, showing glassy on the denim, making it stiff and unwrinkled. I knew this kind of spot; a calf being separated from his breakfast had nuzzled the overalls with his slobbery nose. I wondered what Miss Spurns thought of this man looking and smelling dirty.

Next to me sat Mr. Killpack, the hotel manager, who was there in blue serge, smelling like good cigars. On my other side was the principal, looking like a principal, and next to him Miss Gray with a faint, stony smile as always, as unruffled as an unused swimming pool. And next to her sat Miss Spurns.

The chairman began talking about the reasons for calling the meeting, and after a short time he said, "We regret, Miss Spurns, that the necessity has arisen to inform you that certain people of the community accuse you of violation of two points in the Idaho school law, that dealing with teaching religion in the classroom and that regarding moral behavior. We have asked you and others to this meeting, not to call in question the revocation of your contract as is rumored, but to learn the facts regarding these charges and thereby establish a better relationship between the people of the community and the teachers." He looked from Miss Spurns to members of the board as if to get their approval of his statement of the case.

The charge of teaching religion in the classroom became the first topic of discussion. Somehow, this matter seemed unimportant to me. I thought that most of what Miss Spurns had taught was Christianity, an adjunct and not a challenge to my religion.

Too soon Mr. Brussels was speaking, through stubbled face and uneven yellow teeth, about his children bringing home reports of the teacher having attacked the revelations of God. He would rather his children would remain unschooled, totally illiterate, than have their testimonies destroyed.

"What have you to say regarding these reports, Miss Spurns?" Mr. Hatch asked.

"I have nothing to say except that I have tried to answer questions honestly that have arisen in class."

Mr. Hatch turned to me. "We asked you here, young man" (I was frightened—how could I talk? What could I say before my teachers, and these men?), "we have asked you here, Thomas, to give a report representing the students of the school. Has Miss Spurns in your opinion attacked the principles of the church?"

"Only in the way she said," I answered.

"In answering questions which arise," asked Mr. Hatch, "has she attacked the church?"

"Not exactly," I answered without further comment. Others in the group now spoke, relieving me of the necessity to say more, and leaving my emotions stirring sufficiently to dull my hearing as to what occurred subsequently. Then out of the chaos of my mind I heard Mr. Davis's voice saying: "—a faith which may seem peculiar to you, Miss Spurns, and undoubtedly as you hear fragments of it from the students it appears illogical. When you see it all it makes a better pattern. I do not believe that you have openly attacked our faith; you have not treated this important subject with the delicacy something so sacred to us deserves."

"I am sorry if I have erred in this way, Mr. Davis," Miss Spurns said.

"If we are crude," he continued, "that is not the fault of our religion. Many of our people have risen from total illiteracy, from complete ignorance, to become responsible citizens, happy self-respecting people. Our religion is a vital faith that inspires great loyalty, great action, great sacrifice. It teaches us to seek all truth; that is why we established this little high school and hired you—just because we want our children to have some of the culture you have to offer."

"Mr. Davis has stated our position very well," said the chairman. "We tell you this to let you know that we want your cooperation to preserve all the good things we have."

"Thank you, Mr. Hatch," said the teacher.

"If you think, Miss Spurns," Mr. Davis said, "that our lives in this isolated community are barren, just think how much more barren they would have been had our people not come out of the darkness of disbelief and accepted some of the marvelous light of Christ."

"Do you feel, Miss Spurns," asked Mr. Hatch, "that to ask you to avoid discussions of points of theological doctrine would be in any way unfair?"

"I do not. I shall follow your advice, gentlemen."

"We are concerned with accusations of immoral behavior," the chairman continued, "loose conduct—entertaining men in your room at the hotel."

"But now," he said, turning to me, "we will excuse you, Thomas. Thank you for coming."

I left, feeling as if I had been arbitrated out of adult status to childhood and at a time when it violated my arduous wish. I could now only speculate on what Mr. Killpack, the hotel manager, would report. I had heard my mother say that gullible gossips were spreading the tales, and that Miss Spurns, a city girl, was no doubt finding it hard to adjust to country life. The boys her age were off to war; there was nothing to do at night for relaxation from the treadmill of schoolteaching but to sit in the hotel lobby with a motley assortment of old men talking muffled talk through cuds of chewing tobacco, punctuating conversation with whistling shots at the spittoon, or, the other alternative, to fraternize with bachelor cowboys from Jackson's Hole.

Outside, I walked mopingly to join classmates at school, feeling angry, though I hardly knew why.

Back at school I found the students gathered in the auditorium in unusual unity.

"Are they going to can her?" they chorused.

I did not want to talk. "No," I said curtly, "no case against her. They are advising her, telling her what to do."

"We knew it," Nephi Boseman said, "so we're gon'ta put her out ourselves; we've all signed a petition that we won't go to school if she stays."

"All?" I asked.

"All but Charlie and June."

Charlie and June, I thought; I am with them—stubborn Charlie and prudish June.

"You gotta sign now," Nephi said; "you know what she is."

"Yes, I know what she is, and it's not what you make her with your lies," I said. "I will not sign that paper."

Shouts of protest came from every side. Someone said, "He wants to keep Spurns. Can you believe it?"

Virginia spoke as noise diminished. "Please sign it, Thomas. We want you to sign last because you are president."

I felt a stir in my heart. Another weight was being laid on the scales. In the meeting, I had felt that I was Miss Spurns's advocate and defender. Now I must reject her or be rejected by my peers. Momentarily I felt as if I could not endure isolation from classmates. They were urging, arguing, insisting that I sign.

"All right! All right! I'll do it," I said.

I took the petition and signed. The gadflies had driven me to an impetuous act of conformity.

As I did so, I hardly contemplated the consequence. My youthful idealism led me to conclude unthinkingly that justice somehow would prevail. The school board, the parents, the principal would not listen to a foolish petition initiated by children. If I were a child to be expelled from a meeting, I was a child to be ignored in this. Miss Spurns would stay despite the petition; it would be disregarded.

When the teachers entered the chapel a few minutes later, the students sat orderly and silent, tense in quietness.

The clock marked seconds vocally while the teachers took their seats behind the pulpit. Directly behind Miss Spurns from where I sat and above her head hung the painting of *The Sacred Grove*, the green landscape and trees contrasting with her red hair, a painting of the very place where God told Joseph Smith that all the churches had gone astray.

The principal arose and began, "Students, we are happy to announce that all the teachers have complete support of the school board and that school will continue as usual."

Nephi stood at his seat in the audience. "I got a paper to give ya," he shouted as he started toward the front.

The principal accepted and read the paper silently. My heart pumped loudly in my ears.

"What can this petition mean?" the principal said.

"It means," shouted Nephi, "just what it says; we don't go to school if Spurns stays."

Miss Spurns reached for the petition. She looked at it coldly, intensely; she arose, moved like smoke to the pulpit, and spoke quietly, her eyes piercing. "You are against me, too—I never would have gone through the ignominy I have just experienced had I known that you, my students, were against me."

I could not lift my eyes for shame. I felt alone, an isolate, a sinner condemned by the infallible judge Truth, an inarticulate before his confessor. When I could raise my eyes, Miss Spurns had turned her head and seemed to be looking at *The Sacred Grove*.

Three hours later, before anyone—the principal, the school board, or the parents—had risen to defend the teacher, and before I recovered from the shock of fast-paced action, the mixed train puffed northward carrying Miss Spurns somewhere beyond the valley.

At home that night when I went to my room, I saw Miss Spurns's green book, *Othello*, lying on my dresser, a sardonic accuser, telling me of my own perfidy.

CHAPTER
7

World War I, 1917–1918

GEORGE SMITH

I n 1915 World War I was raging in Europe. George Smith, second son of Albert and Mary Ann Smith, lived with his parents and siblings on a farm at the foot of the mountains on the south end of the valley. The Smith ditch taken out of the String Canal supplied the Smith farm with plentiful water to irrigate their fertile farm. The Smith family, like other farm families, planted every arable acre of land and followed the best-known procedures to produce food for friendly countries at war.

When the *Lusitania* was sunk in May 1915, by German submarines skulking on the bottom of the sea, people in Victor were outraged, as was all America. The *Denver Post*, with bold headlines, vivid pictures, and fiery words about the brutal drowning of 1,198 men, women, and children, voyagers on a passenger ship sailing in neutral waters, ignited a fire in patriotic hearts, and tempers exploded. The Smith family shared in this contagious outrage.

As President Wilson and other diplomats worked to keep our country out of war and Germany yielded for a time to demands to desist from submarine warfare, tempers cooled. George Smith and other young men like him, however, kept the fire of revenge smoldering until two years later when the Germans resumed submarine warfare, sinking U.S. Merchant Marine ships.

Our embroilment in this war became overwhelming, and on April 6, 1917, Congress declared war, joining with allied forces.

Later, in December, a Pathé newsreel, presented in a movie at Rice Hall in Victor, showed the story of a volunteer soldier, the popular mayor of Idaho Falls, George W. Eddington. The silent movie showed him standing on the steps of the public library dressed in the uniform of a United States Army officer, then moving to lead about one hundred recruits in a parade through the streets of the town. Captions on the screen praised the mayor and the recruits for giving up the comforts of home to serve their country.

George Smith saw this film. Late one evening, sitting with other men by a potbellied stove in the pool hall, he heard Ben Jones read from the *Idaho Falls Daily Post* an account of the farewell celebration held on December 12th, honoring Mayor Eddington and the recruits. C. E. Dinwoody had given an address in which he said to the departing soldiers:

"You are the chosen ones, the flower of manhood, the best fitted to fight for liberty. This is no time to be half-hearted or lukewarm, but a time for wholehearted, fiery valor. You volunteers are the valorous ones. You show your colors by your deeds."

George Smith decided to enlist. A man of twenty-three, he had stayed at home and worked on the farm. He appeared to be as carefree as a cow in a pasture or a dog with a bone. As unpolished as Huck Finn and as uncomfortable as Huck in church or school, George had grown up, a curly-headed, inoffensive product of nature. If his rusticity, his dowdy dress, his uncouth language repulsed you, his geniality and complete absence of guile would impress you.

George told his mother he was going to enlist in the army.

"You won't," she said. "I did not raise my boy to kill in battle or be killed."

George avoided bringing unhappiness to anyone. He listened to his mother, and for a time stayed on the farm. The next spring the draft came and George was forced to register for military service.

"You can get a release, an exemption," his mother said. "You can serve the war effort by producing food on the farm."

George refused to apply for exemption. Then in May he and eight other young men of our town responded to the call to military duty.

When this occurred, the community planned a gala farewell. Emotions ran high for the occasion. Never had the Rice Hall been so overcrowded, never was "The Star Spangled Banner" sung with more feeling, never was the flag saluted with more devotion, never did young men wear the army uniform with more pride than that night, and rarely did John D. Killpack deliver such a fiery address. William Cullen Bryant or Senator William E. Borah could not have done better.

He said: "President Wilson has been patient, we have turned the other cheek, we have pleaded in diplomatic voice for safe passage in the seas—and have been ignored! Kaiser Wilhelm is a tyrant, a despot. He grinds his grizzly teeth in lust to devour democracy."

As he concluded the oration, he carved every word carefully before he let it fall: "We will prevail! We will crush the Huns! These our boys who are going into battle go with pride to serve their country and their God. They will return."

These last words made the saliva flow. It was a masterful oration.

A few days later the nine soldier boys boarded the train. At the station a massive crowd shed tears and shouted cheers as the train whistle blew and the train puffed away.

In following months the reality of the war came home so vividly to people of the valley that imaginative ears and eyes could hear and see the battles. The pool hall, the barbershop, the blacksmith shop, the livery stable received and dispensed war news. The people prayed for peace. The Relief Society collected grease, made quilts, knit sweaters, and, to save scarce foods, planned appropriate menus. At gatherings in a gayer mood crowds sang, "Goodbye, Broadway, Hello, France," and "The Yanks are coming, the Yanks are coming, the drums rum-tumming everywhere." That was the time when every ear was tuned to the middle C, every eye on the same star, and every heart beating to the same drummer.

No one complained about "Hooverizing"—following the Herbert Hoover–directed Food Administration's pleas to observe meatless, wheatless, sweetless days for the war effort. The President, to encourage food production, had promised $2.26 a bushel for wheat, over three times the normal price. The profit motive now, with will-to-win-the-war, moved like an equally matched team of work horses to pull the load and produce an unprecedented wheat crop.

The Smith family fought the battle on the home front with girls and children plowing, planting, irrigating, and harvesting crops.

When Albert Smith had to answer the question "How is George?" he could answer only, "Don't know—letters scarce as hen's teeth!" When the Smiths did get a letter, farmers meeting on a road in their wagons stopped to call "Whoa" to their horses and say, "Did you hear? Smiths got a letter from George today. They are shipping him over. He's going to help pay our debt to France."

Although George Smith could spin off words in substandard English as fast as a buzz saw in a sawmill, his writing moved, according to Albert, "slow as cold tar. He told us," said Albert, "to use his whole name in addressing letters along with his number, for in his unit were eleven George Smiths, and in the shipload to go across would be a thousand George Smiths and a hundred George Anthony Smiths."

In October long lists in newspapers of American men killed in action stunned the nerve-tense nation. Now four million American men were mobilized and half were overseas. The *Denver Post* reported, "The American Army is engaged in a vicious battle in the Argonne Forest—the greatest battle as an independent unit of Americans ever assembled in battle. This rough backland which nature has made easily defensible, the Germans have made almost impregnable by use of networks of trenches seven miles thick protected by barbed-wire-fence entanglements and camouflaged concrete pits of machine-gun emplacements. This our fighting men are conquering—but not without enormous casualties. The best blood of America is staining the trenches of the Argonne."

The report came that Scott Humble had been wounded in battle. Days later George Murdock received a telegram, the well-known official one beginning, "We regret to inform you . . ." His brother, Lynn, had been killed in action.

The Smith family waited in the front line of the fearful ones watching, hoping, praying for George's safety. Where was he? Was he in Argonne Forest, crouching like a badger in earth holes looking for a groundhog? Was he killing the Huns or being killed?

The harvest was over now. Children in the upper grades who had been released to help in the harvest had returned to school. The pool hall, closed for harvest in daytime, was again open. Albert and Mary Ann Smith had grown weary of worry. "George will survive," said Albert. "If he is in battle, he will use his good eyes. He is careful enough to be steady in aim. He could win the prize in target shooting before he joined the army."

"He is a good boy," said his mother. "God will protect him."

Albert returned home from town on November 4th. "No letter from George," he said to his wife.

"He never writes!" Mary Ann answered sadly.

"Good news," said Albert. "They say in town that the long, long battle for the Argonne is almost over—that the war will soon be won."

He had hardly spoken when a knock came at the door.

"You must have followed me from town," Albert said.

"I have a telegram," the boy said. "Came in at the depot."

No one spoke. All were silent—silent in fear. Albert opened the letter. Mary Ann and he stared at the paper. A tear rolled down Mary Ann's cheek. Albert read slowly, ". . . inform you that your son, George Anthony Smith, was killed . . ." He choked and handed the telegram to his wife. After a time she said, "Our son is not dead. It is another George Anthony Smith. Remember there are others by that name."

When whistles blew and bells rang in a day and night celebration of the signing of the Armistice a week later, the Smiths could hardly smile.

"For us," said Albert, "the barn was locked *after* the horse escaped."

Mary Ann held to a lingering, yet weakening, hope that her George was alive, that another Smith had fallen in his stead, until a package of his belongings came. Among other things was a snapshot of her he had kept, and with it a sculptured relief likeness of her cut in an inch-thick block of wood about the size of a postcard. He had carved it with a pocketknife from the snapshot and from memory.

CHAPTER 8

Twentieth-Century Plague, 1918–1919

THE DOCTOR

T he gaiety of the November 11th celebration of the Armistice ending the war died away into quiet darkness like that following a fireworks show. A new horror equal to that of the war spread in the land. The *Denver Post*, with blazing headlines, pictures, and stories of the deadly influenza epidemic, filled the people of the valley with unrelenting fear. Medical science could find no successful medication, no control, no effective treatment, and no means to prevent the spread of this fast and furious killer disease. It spread faster than a prairie fire, killing thousands of its victims in every city, town, and hamlet it reached. Could the people of Teton Valley escape the infection? Could they improve upon the natural isolation of the valley to shut out the elusive virus?

A young graduate from medical school came to our town that year and set up practice. All of the people, even the older ones who held complete confidence in him in suspension until he proved himself, were delighted to have a doctor in town.

While people of the valley were ringing alarm bells in each other's ears of the westward advance of the disease, the young doctor made ready. With calm self-composure he faced his personal danger, knowing that his duty and his oath of office would demand exposure to the virus and immerse him in its infection. Then the deeply concerned Southern Idaho chapter of the American Medical Association called a conference in Idaho Falls of physicians to dispense the limited knowledge available on treatment of the disease. As the young doctor boarded the train to go to the conference, he said in jest to a friend, "I will probably bring the disease back with me when I return and die of it."

A week later he came home, went to bed, and awoke the next morning with a hot fever. Shortly half the families in the town lay sick, victims of influenza. The doctor served none of them, for he died, the first fatality of the "flu" in Teton Valley.

THE BLACKSMITH

Willie Thompson's blacksmith shop stood near the cottonwoods that marked the route of Trail Creek. Day after day, week after week, year after year Willie lived a life of strenuous labor. He did not look strong; in fact, he looked rather slight; yet, in shoeing a mean workhorse he could hold up a fourth of its weight. An iron man was he. He could curse the horses in language they understood as well as pet them to calm them down. The only rest we ever saw him take from shoeing horses, pumping the forge, feeding the fire, swinging the heavy sledge to sharpen a plowshare or mend machinery was to roll and light a cigarette.

When the armistice was signed ending the war, joy seemed to explode in the hearts of all the people. To amplify their joy, Willie felt a need to provide a fitting initiation for the armistice celebration. He tipped the heavy anvil up from its metal base, filled the opening, about the size of a matchbox, with gunpowder, threaded a fuse to it through an aperture, tipped the anvil up again to fit tightly over the metal plate. At daylight on November 11, 1918, Willie lit the fuse and the ignited powder blew the anvil flying, its blast breaking the air with a boom that rattled the windows and aroused the town. By the dawn's early light the celebration had begun. The revelry continued several days before community life returned to normal. Then one day Jim Berger took his bobsled to the blacksmith shop to have a runner repaired. As Willie worked, Jim said, "I heard that Doc has brought the flu to town."

"Ya, it's scary as hell," said Willie.

"Sure is," said Jim. "I haven't thought much about religion and death, but now it's kinda pushin' me."

"It makes a man think," said Willie, "but the Bible-reading people expect us to be too good. Christ was good. They killed him. They'll kill us if we're too good."

"Are you going to close shop and hide out from the contagion?" asked Jim.

"No! Can't afford it," said Willie. "Got to keep bread on the table for the wife and kids."

Ironically, the flu infection must have already invaded Willie's body when he talked to Jim, for the next day he closed shop—went home with the chills.

People had pulled into their homes like turtles pulling heads into shells for protection. We did not know how the Thompson family met the enemy until a grave was being dug for Essie, Willie's wife.

When Essie was buried, bitter-cold days and colder nights thickened the ice on creeks and river. Willie, still fighting infection, could not ride through the bitter wind to the cemetery. Then came snow day after day. Yet, by the time Willie could fire the forge again, the blasting wind, the bitter cold, and blinding snow had all moderated. Willie, not yet in full strength and not his usual self, talked with customers only as necessity demanded. Then, as the mood changed through the healing power of time, he talked. "I got pneumonia," he said. "It plugged up my lungs. It burned my brains out. All I could hear was that cursed jazz song, '*Over there, over there*—the Yanks are comin' . . . the drums rum-tummin' everywhere.' Them damn drums poundin' louder and louder and louder. I went to hell. 'Essie!' I yelled, 'shut off that damned phonograph.' She just stood there and looked at me—said nothing. I yelled again, 'Shut off that god-damned phonograph'—an' she stood there like a statue. 'Damn you, Essie,' I said in my madness. Then I passed out. When I come out of it, she was dead. I cursed her! That is the hell of it all!"

DIGGING ALTA'S GRAVE

The town council acted quickly when influenza invaded the privacy of our valley that November. They closed the schools, which had just settled into routine, and forbade all public gatherings. In those days we willingly obeyed announcements and suggestions on avoidance of exposure—stayed by our own fires, never visited neighbors, never shopped or entered a public building except when dire necessity demanded it.

Our school superintendent, David E. Williams, along with his administrative duties, taught algebra, chemistry, physics, carpentry, and animal husbandry—and managed to drop words of wisdom along the way. Now, with school closed, he and his twelve teachers were temporarily out of work.

One day Mr. Williams knocked at our door and asked if I could help dig a grave. The sexton and his family, like the majority of families along Trail Creek, were stricken with flu. Nine people in our little community had died in five days. The living must bury the dead.

The principal got two other boys of his high school with picks and shovels and we dug a grave for our deceased classmate, Alta Sinclair. As we started to dig, Arden Stevans said, "Mr. Williams, yesterday this earth and rock was hard as hell. Last night it froze. How hard is it now?"

"Hard as the gates of hell," Mr. Williams answered. "They hold the devils in."

As two dug in the three-foot by six-foot hole while two rested, our conversation often turned to the mystery of death. At times we became reverently serious as we shared the fear and horror of the killer epidemic that stalked us day and night. "Someone may be digging a grave for one of us next," one said.

We all fell quiet until Mr. Williams said, " 'The door of death is made of gold / That mortal eyes cannot behold.' Blake said that," he continued. "You see what it means, don't you?"

LOUIS HUFF

Louis Huff's father was Hyrum Hale. His mother died giving birth to a sister two years younger than he. Hyrum Hale gave his three little children away for adoption. Charles and Emma Huff adopted Louis, their only child.

Louis wiggled his way through childhood, active as a cat on coals. The Huffs fed him, clothed him, sheltered him, pampered him, and spoiled him. In school he pushed and pestered other pupils until they petered out; he scribbled on their papers, pulled their hair, chased them through aisles and halls until teachers were irritated, agitated, aggravated, and completely exasperated. Then he grew up to be a handsome, happy, articulate, confident, carefree youth.

A pretty girl, Erma, caught his gaze, brought his smile, loosened his tongue. He followed her in, he followed her out, and caught her behind the door. When Erma's father found that she was going to be a mother, he figuratively went out with his shotgun to bring Lou in to make him marry her, but he couldn't find him. Louis had left the valley.

Winter came, and with its winds the lethal flu swept the country and laid the people low. In the midst of the epidemic, word came from the Snake River country that Louis Huff had died. The sick, the dying, and the dead at the time demanded attention and sapped the energies of the able-bodied ones. They could not ship Louis's body home.

THE CHRISTMAS I MISSED

Two days before Christmas in 1918 my schoolteacher sister, Naomi, came home from the lower valley, where she had attended a teacher's meeting, and went to bed ill. In November, flu had swept through our town, but the Cheney family had escaped.

On the morning of December 24th, as Naomi lay sick with what we called a "cold," we prepared for Christmas. Mother and I got up early, for work was to be done to make Christmas merry. I built a fire in the range and brought in more wood. While Mother cooked goodies, I would get a Christmas tree from the canyon.

I saddled Old White, my pony, strapped the axe to the right side of the saddle, and galloped off for a two-mile ride to the foothills where trees were plentiful. Though snow covered the ground and refrigerated the air, the sun was warm, my coat thick, and my heart happy. I had found a pretty tree and had started for home, carrying it across the saddle in front of me, when suddenly I shivered and felt cold. It was a sudden chill like jumping into the pond, and I was so tired, I wanted to lie down.

Plez Sherman's haystack, close to the road, had been cut on the south end with a hay knife, and the shelf of dry, green hay about four feet high, catching the warmth of the sun, invited me. I dismounted from my horse, threw the reins over a post of the stackyard fence, stood the tree by the fence, and climbed on the hay, shaking with cold. I lay where the sun concentrated its rays against the wall of hay, protected from the wintry breeze. The sun warmed me. How long I rested I do not know. I wanted to stay there but I knew I could not, for I was sick at heart and must get home.

As I climbed off the hay and went for my horse, I saw that she had two heads that moved in unison and then amalgamated into one. On her back again and starting toward home with the tree across the saddle, I urged her to a gallop, for I felt a need to hurry. My head swam, however, until I felt insecure, and I reined her to a walk. I could not hold the tree; I let it fall by the roadside. My only concern now was to get home. To keep myself from falling, I leaned over and clung to my pony's neck with the saddle horn digging into my chest. As that became unbearable, I would sit up and grip the saddle horn. Then I would drop to the pony's neck again and say, "White, take me home."

I remember little of what happened when I got home or immediately afterward. All I remember is that sometime later I awoke and my sister Cora sat by my bed with tears in her eyes.

"Is it Christmas morning?" I asked.

Cora smiled as she wiped a tear away and said, "No, yesterday was Christmas. You missed it."

"Where are Mother and the rest?" I asked.

"Mother is very sick in her room—and Naomi and Stenna are sick in their room—and little Gordon is very sick with Mother."

She stopped, silent in tears.

"Why are you crying?" I asked. "Are you sick?"

"I am not sick," she said, "but you have been very, very sick, and I am happy you can talk sensibly. You have been delirious—talked so out-of-your-head. We can't get help—no doctor—people are afraid to come in. I am alone with all of you so sick."

"You did not have a Christmas tree," I said.

"No one cared about a Christmas tree," she said.

MATTIE STEVENS

Nathan Stevens with his wife, Mattie, and six children lived on their farm at the mouth of Trail Creek Canyon. Their fourth child and oldest son, Nate, grew up with a natural charisma—a winning smile, contagious laughter, and ready wit. He matured, a churchgoing youth who accepted a call and served his church for two years as a missionary. He returned home, a joy to the community and the pride of his mother. Then capricious fate cut him down; pneumonia burned him up with fever, then laid him cold in death.

Mattie's despair at her son's death became a lasting grief. After his burial she walked a mile each day to the cemetery, sat by the grave for hours, and wept. As her depression grew, she neglected her living children and her personal instinct of self-preservation and, unheedful of storm and cold of winter, she sat at the graveside day after day. People first empathized, then sympathized, and, finally, when the tempo of her grief did not abate, pitied her.

Mrs. Sweet, the nearest neighbor, kept a watchful eye on Mattie, advised her, and shared concern for her welfare with her husband and children. When spring came and Mattie's grief had not subsided, Mrs. Sweet was getting short on patience. It was then that Frank, Mattie's youngest son, knocked at her door. "Come quick," he said, "Mama can't stand to live any longer. She is going to jump into the river."

It was warm now; spring runoff filled Trail Creek until its water lapped over its banks as it dashed through the Stevens's backyard. Mrs. Sweet ran to the rescue and found the two oldest daughters physically holding Mattie as she struggled to reach the river.

Calmly Mrs. Sweet said, "Let go, girls!" They obeyed. "Now, Mattie," she said emphatically, "Go—jump into the river. It is exactly what you need. It will cool off the heat of your stupid grieving, and wash some sense into your skull."

Mattie stood amazed without moving.

"Go on," said Mrs. Sweet. "See how it feels to jump into that icy water."

Mattie did not jump into the river, nor did she ever again threaten to do so. That day she began to recover.

CHAPTER 9

Romance and Regret, 1916–1922

Florence McDonald

After a pretended struggle, the sixth-grade boy gave up the paper to Florence, of course, and she read the words "I love you" that he had written there. She raised her eyes slowly to his and said, "You're soft . . . and . . ." and, after a pause, smiled and added softly, "and sweet." Then she ran swiftly away as if to escape from words she should not have spoken.

Two years later, in the eighth grade, the commitment of that boy to that girl found expression in little bouquets of flowers picked from his mother's garden, bashfully given and joyfully received.

In any game or contest at school in which pupils selected a classmate, Florence always won the vote. She was loved by every eighth-grade boy, but the one who brought the flowers gained her love.

Then the inevitable happened. When graduation time came, Florence had grown taller than the boy and her dark eyes and wavy brown hair adorned her shapely femininity. In fact, while the boys of the class still sang soprano and wore knickers, the girls became women.

A handsome young man of twenty, Leo Hutchings, had come to Teton Basin and with new buggy, new harness, and team gained the attention that such a one receives from star-struck girls. He chose Florence, the darling of the eighth-grade graduating class, and she chose him. Now, at this turn of events, her childhood lover stretched his neck and tried to talk in low tones to usher in adolescence, all to no avail.

Florence was nature's child and passion's bride, an Annabel Lee made to love and be loved. That autumn she became Leo's bride, his joy, his prize, his triumph. But the light that draws the moth often burns its wings. Down from the transcendental light of mystery came love into a world of responsibility. Too soon the lovers became parents, and Florence, so recently out of the cradle, rocked it. Leo had no means of support. Even the buggy and horses belonged to his father. Now unable to dip into the family treasure, he took the only work available—he became a coal miner in the mine east of Driggs and moved with his wife and child into a one-room log cabin next to a half dozen like it deep in the wooded canyon at the mouth of the mine. In the camp lived two other women, both middle-aged, buxom, and uncouth, as different from Florence as mountain cats from a kitten.

While Leo worked long days in the mine, Florence watched the baby with worrisome love that made every whimper a fear and every cry a warning. Alone in winter with the baby all day, she fed firewood and coal to the stove to keep warm. Alone in winter snow, she carried water in a pail from a spring a quarter mile away, heated it in a boiler on the stove, and washed diapers on a washboard in the round, galvanized tub. All day long, every day the same, until after dark Leo would come home, now metamorphosed from her Don Juan into a lowly miner with coal-dust-dustied face, hands, and clothes. Yet he greeted her with the same voice and the same heartfelt devotion. Before washing away the dirt, he would saw and chop kindling wood and carry it to the woodbox for fire for another day. After cleaning up, he rarely found Florence or himself able to recapture any of the luster of a year before.

Soon came a night when these inexperienced parents met the very embodiment of their fears. The baby's snuffles became croup, and they struggled through a frightful night of breathless fear at every dire gasp of their sick baby. The next day Leo left work to make a day's trek in a bobsled to take his wife and baby to her mother's home.

As Leo drove back to the mine that evening, he could not remove from his mind a fear, an apprehension, a foreboding. Something Florence had said in bidding him good-bye sounded so final. The farewell kiss, though warm and tender, seemed to be the plucking of the flower. And she had said, "Thank God I am away from that lonely cabin. I am so sorry for you, Leo, for now you will be alone."

Now with her baby in the security of her mother's experience and care, Florence felt released from fear. She felt as if she had awakened from a bad dream. In the mountain cabin an overwhelming melancholy had imprisoned her. The wind in the trees at the cabin had become a song of despair. She knew she could never return.

LEO HUTCHINGS

Months had passed since Leo's young wife, Florence, with the sick baby, had left the cabin at the mine and failed to return. Leo had accepted the pick and shovel and damp darkness of the mine to support his sweetheart wife and child. He wanted desperately to preserve the treasure of their love. Although since leaving she had repeatedly declared that her love for him was dead, he did not, he could not accept it. How could a love that had so verdantly blossomed, been so powerfully expressed in word and deed, die so suddenly? Her eye, her tongue, her touch—every element of her soul had been her signature on his valentine of love. Out of his despondent heart he continued to climb the ladder of hope, to search in the corners of his mind for a way to recharge her battery of love.

One Saturday in autumn Leo went home from the mine to his parents in Victor. He knew that if he knocked at the McDonalds' door no one would let him in. He knew also that his gregarious and vivacious wife of seventeen might attend the dance that night. At his home his mother, aware of his despondency, honored his taciturnity and early that evening bade him goodbye as he went away cleaned and dressed for the dance. She did not ask why he left long before dance time. He went from the farmhouse at the mouth of Pole Canyon north to town and turned east toward the McDonald home northeast of town at the base of the mountain. Darkness shielded his approach. He drove up a logging road up the mountainside to the east and circled back in the forest edge. Back from the McDonald home in the forest he left his buggy and walked toward the house. As he approached a window on the north side of the house through which light came around the edges of a blind, a door around the corner opened. Leo crouched in silence. Delbert, Florence's younger brother, came out and went to the barn. Leo went to the window and peeped through the crack at the bottom of the blind. The room was empty. Shortly he heard a buggy coming from the barnyard. Through the window he caught a glimpse of Florence as she went to the door. He knew now that Delbert had prepared the buggy to take Florence to the dance. Leo stole away in the darkness and watched as Florence got into the buggy.

Local dance patrons took pride in their five-piece dance orchestra: a piano, a violin, a trumpet, a saxophone, and drums. This ensemble could loosen feet and lighten hearts. Young people came out of the woods and backlands to dance, and older people came to look and listen.

Leo entered the hall as the orchestra played lustily. Florence was already dancing, dancing with a man Leo did not know. Someone asked, "Leo, did you bring your wife to the dance?"

Leo looked at him with a stoic face and did not answer. When the orchestra stopped, Leo walked across the floor to Florence. It was an impulsive act motivated by inner compulsion. As Florence talked pleasantly with other boys, Leo came to the side, unseen by her, took her hand, and turned her gently toward him. She withdrew the hand, her face changing in a moment from carefree fun to fear.

"Florence," he said, "dance with me! Talk to me!"

"Please, Leo," she said, "not now—not here."

"You are my wife," he said. "I have rights."

"No! No! Not here!" she said, and ran away.

Leo glared at the young men standing by, then walked back across the floor to join the crowd of men. Arlo Johnson, who had been watching, said, "Leo, let her go to hell!"

Leo answered through clenched teeth, "She's mine, and I'll go to hell to keep her."

While popular girls danced and less popular girls stood in waiting on the right side of the dance floor, Leo stood on the left side with the men—the shy, the watchers, and the waiters. He did not dance that night. He did not want to dance. Flashes of thoughts of the stuff life is made of crowded feverishly into his head—glory in the moonlight, laughter in the sun, and, conversely, shadows in the path, darkness in defeat, thunder in broken dreams, tempest in the soul. All through the dance he watched Florence in her gaiety, and it burned his tortured soul. Franz Coy, who had worked with him, saw lines of distress in his face and said, "Leo, come home with me! Watching her is dynamite in your head. Come. Let's go!"

"I'll kill him!" Leo said, angered at the flirtatious public display of attention the young man he had observed all night made toward Florence, who accepted and requited it in playful abandon. How desperately Leo wanted to touch her, to be touched by her, to receive her smile. All evening he had watched her smile, and her smile went everywhere except to him. Her beauty, her charm, her graceful ease touched with a trace of melancholy made her a star—the belle of the ball.

The orchestra played a slow waltz. Florence and the man danced in loving embrace. The fuse in Leo's brain had burned out; the explosion came. He burst into action. He dodged through dancers on the floor, clutched the man by the shoulders, and tore him away from Florence. "Leave my wife alone!" he shouted as he pulled his strong right arm back with clenched fist. Others moved away. The floor manager ran to the scene and grabbed Leo's arm.

"Come outside!" Leo called to his adversary.

Dancers on the floor said, "A fight—a fight!" as they followed the men and the floor manager out the door.

In such dance-hall quarrels self-appointed referees always took charge to assure fair play. Outside on the grass people gathered in a circle, and at the referee's signal the fistfight began. Neither Leo nor his opponent had had any training in fistfighting and no more in experience than boyhood battles. But tonight Leo was the lion, the maddened animal. His muscles hardened by toil and his temper tight in anger led him to strike telling blows. The opponent fell to be called out in the first short round.

Out of this triumph, however, came the greater defeat, for it widened the gulf between Leo and his estranged wife. The strength of the arm could win a fair lady in medieval times, but this was the twentieth century. He lost her. Leo's time of glory in the flower had gone forever.

Clara Driggs

Lovely Clara Driggs accepted an invitation to be my date for the traditional New Year's dance. We arrived at the hall full of youthful energy to bring the New Year into our lives with frolicking joy. At first we moved around, filling our dance programs, greeting and exchanging dances with friends, saving the first, midnight, and last dances for ourselves. I loved to dance. I knew the joys of other active winter sports—skating, skiing, coasting, sleigh riding—but nothing even touched the joy of dancing. It was a feeling, an emotion that rose in voltage, differing in its power with one or another partner. The variety of response to the dance provided the spice. The stimulating girls entertained me, the special ones entranced me. There was the buxom farm girl, Charlotte, bold and forceful, who stole the lead from me, danced like a drummer in perfect rhythm beating and booming with the whole body; there was the scholar, Virginia, whose charm lay more in her stimulating conversation than in her agility on the dance floor. With her I did not care if she missed a beat or if I had to twist on a heel to miss her foot. There was the clinging vine, Winnie, who grasped me in such a vigorous and possessive embrace that we moved as if we were one four-legged animal whose feet missed each other as if coordinated with the same brain. In her clasp I at times would push away to relieve my fear that the floor manager might tap me on the shoulder to remind me of dance-floor etiquette. There was the Nutcracker ballerina, the dancing doll, Imo, who floated like a Christmas sprite in unity with me like my shadow. There was the natural, Emma, born with dancing feet, matured with feminine charm—every movement a dance. I responded to the tender touch of her hand, to her softness, to the velvet touch of her dress. Then there was Clara, my choice that night for any dance, the fox trot, two-step, or waltz.

The midnight hour approached. "The New Year is near!" shouted the orchestra leader. "Take your partner for the dance."

Ushers passed out balloons, noisemakers, and little bags of confetti. I found Clara, she took my arm, and we waited as seconds ticked away. The hall door opened and with the boom of the shooting off of the anvil, announcing the midnight hour, pandemonium broke loose—shouts of

Happy New Year everywhere, noisemakers, laughter, drums beating, and with it all a flutter of multicolored confetti interspersed with colorful balloons flying in the air. As the New Year hysteria reached its climax, I put an arm around Clara. She rose up on her toes and gave me a special New Year's gift: a kiss.

About one o'clock we came to the last number on the program. Clara and I took the dance embrace with a burst of delight—she the sweetest sixteen, the Juliet in my life, and now my hand a glove on her hand. How charming her movement! How lithely she followed my lead! We danced off into a dream of tranquility, transported into the bliss of motion and emotion, swinging in the clouds above reality, everthing else lost. The orchestra played the waltz as we followed its rhythm. "It's three o'clock in the morning. We've danced the whole night through . . . I could just keep right on dancing forever, dear, with you." But, sadly, the strains of music faded, and the reality of the cold night entered the hall as open doors let in the blast of winter.

As we reached Clara's door, she said, "You must come in. I made a huckleberry pie for us."

Inside I opened the drafts on the heater and put wood on the coals while Clara prepared the pie. Soon the fire blazed, the pine wood spit, and heat threatened to destroy the artwork Jack Frost had painted on the window-panes.

As we ate the delicious pie, we talked with animation about the dance, friends, and school. I had come home from school at Rexburg for the holidays, while Clara attended Victor High School. She and two other girls from the west side of the valley had rented a small house for the school year.

"Kate and Caroline, my roommates, did not have dates for the dance tonight," Clara said, "so the house is mine."

"Alone?" I said. "Are you afraid of wolves?"

She took my hand and said sweetly, "I am not alone. You are with me."

FERN ALLRED

Fern was eighteen going on nineteen when I met her that pleasant June evening. I had driven my Model T out of the valley to Rexburg, where we met at Mrs. Mortensen's boardinghouse. A genial hostess, Mrs. Mortensen put Fern Allred, Maurita Cleveland, Ralph Reese, and me at ease when we met there for dinner. As we sat at the huge dining table, the hostess said, "There will be fourteen around this table tomorrow, eleven girls and three men."

"Eleven girls!" I said. "Wow!"

"A paradise for men," she continued. Then she added, "You two girls make the best of your head start with these men."

Maurita laughed, Fern smiled.

Then Mrs. Mortensen explained, "These two girls are special; they are from Paris."

"Paris, Idaho," Fern said.

Smiling, Mrs. Mortensen continued, "Fern's father has his brand on more beef cattle than any other man in these parts, and Maurita's father is Sheriff of Bear Lake County."

We ate that meal in pleasant conversation neither restrained nor animated. I saw Reese watching Maurita as light from the setting sun tiptoed on her wavy hair, highlighting its amber loveliness. He said, "Daughter of the sheriff, eh, gun-toting keeper of the peace? Does he catch the horse thieves and bank robbers?"

"No," Maurita said, "my dad's worry is keeping cattlemen from putting their brand on other ranchers' calves."

I looked at Fern and said, "Does the sheriff do a good job in keeping thieves from branding your dad's calves?"

"My dad rides the range at branding time and the sheriff brings in the thieves," she answered, her dark eyes flashing. The next day we would register for summer school, but tonight we were free. After dinner when the girls had gone to their room, Reese said to me, "Let's take the two girls to a movie tonight."

"I'll ask the blonde," I said.

"I want the blonde," Reese said. "We'll flip a coin," he continued as he dug into his pocket. "You call."

"Heads," I said.

It landed tails. I got the brunette. That marked the beginning. The girl I got by the flip of a coin became my constant date. We not only ate together at the big dining table, we walked from class to class together, we attended school activities, we rode together in my car up and down the Snake River Valley talking all the while of things both trivial and significant. Her mind and heart became my laboratory for research.

That summer we were not lovers in the usual sense. No moonstruck sweethearts we, keeping our relationship on the front burner, whispering sweet nothings in moonlight and roses. I never took my date out to dinner. Why should I? We paid board at Mrs. Mortensen's. I never invited her devotion with sundaes and banana splits as other boys did. But I had a car, a rarity among students. Gasoline took me further with my girl than ice cream. One day as we sat in my Model T, parked on the street not far from a popcorn vendor, Fern said, "That popcorn smells good."

"I'll drive over closer," I said, "so you can smell it better."

School closed, bringing fond farewells. Then came memories, letters, meetings, separations—and romance. And—the final result of the flip of the coin—married life together, in which to my regret my lovely brunette repeatedly reminded me of the popcorn she didn't get.

Will Avery and Farm Life, 1918–1920

EMMA'S STORY UNCONFIRMED

A small, thousand-pound white pony had been turned loose in the Gray's Lake country where she lived and bred with other horses running wild, foraging well in summer and pawing through snow for dry, dead grass for survival in winter. For three generations she had roamed free and bred foals. Her offspring now numbered sixteen horses and colts. Will Avery bought them for a pittance. He and the men from the Austin Ranch had rounded them up and broken in three of the offspring to lead and ride. Dolly, the matriarch of the herd, had already learned the lessons of bridle and saddle. Will Avery and I, a sixteen-year-old youth, took the herd through mountains and valleys about seventy-five miles to Teton Valley. I rode Dolly and led a newly tamed mare named Nell, a daughter of Dolly, carrying a pack-saddle load of supplies. Uncle Will, as I called him, rode a daughter of Dolly, a seven-year-old bay he named Dove, only slightly accustomed to saddle and bridle, and led another partly trained horse, a granddaughter of Dolly, carrying a pack.

From Gray's Lake we went over the mountain and down Tin-Cup Canyon to Star Valley, Wyoming. The horses that we rode and led were instinctively followed by the younger herd.

The first night we stayed at a farm in the vicinity of the town of Freedom, the main street of which marks the dividing line of Idaho and Wyoming. Uncle Will had prearranged for our lodging. As we came out of Tin-Cup Canyon, Uncle Will said to me, "This is a large, prosperous dairy farm where we are staying. They milk about thirty-five Guernsey dairy cows. John, the owner, works hard, and everybody on his farm works hard. His wife died a year or two ago—worked herself to death. Then John said that he couldn't do without help—had to have a wife to keep house for him and his boys, to cook, wash, and clean, and take care of the garden. And do you know what he did? He put an ad in a dairyman's magazine for a wife, asked for what he wanted—a strong woman willing to work, between forty and fifty—and, by my word, he got her."

I was all ears. And I would meet these strange people today, the kind that I thought were only in Horatio Alger's or Charles Dickens's novels.

"Hello, Will," called the dairyman as we came riding in with the parade of horses following. "See ya made it here with them nags. Put 'em in that second pasture to the north and come in to supper, you and that skinny boy you have with ya—looks like he needs grub."

The big man had yelled so loud that our horses all jerked their heads up and swung their ears forward and high to listen. Immediately I respected this man.

We entered a kitchen as big as a schoolroom with table and chairs for a dozen or so. There, working at the kitchen range, stood a buxom woman—a Marjorie Main—looking and acting efficient.

"Will," said the dairyman, "meet my wife, Sadie. Sadie, this is Austin Brothers' foreman, Will Avery, and his helper, Tom—what's your name?"

"We expected ya, Will," said Sadie. "You two just make yourself at home. Get rid of yer hat and chaps and wash yerselves at the basin there on the washstand, and use that clean towel, not the dirty ones the boys have wiped their dirt on."

After supper Uncle Will, John, and I sat on some sacks of feed in the granary room of the cow barn, talking.

"You're going to Teton Valley, are ye, Will?" said John.

"Yes," said Will, "I'm going to marry an old friend who lives there."

"Hitchin' up with one who will pull her share of the load, are ye?"

"He is going to marry my mother," I said.

"Well, well," said John, "let me tell you two somethin'. Ye have ta be damn good, both of ye, if ye get along. If ye ever give that boy hell, Will," he said as he gave me a testy glance, "ye gotta make him like it."

"We'll get by," Will said. "We are going to run his mother's farms—good land like this here—like yours."

"Quitting sheep business for farming," said the dairyman. "That's like movin' out of the house into the barn."

"Tired of it," said Will. "Tired of sheep camps and sourdough bread—want to live at home and eat a good woman's cooking."

"You ain't had it bad with the company, Will," said John, "bein' the manager with big money—they feed ya good grub, bein' the boss."

"True, true," said Will, "but I have headaches—getting good herders, problems with shearing and lambing, selling lambs and wool at the right time for a profit. My work is not all sunshine and gravy. You, John, have about a hundred livestock here to watch. I have eight herds of sheep, about fifteen thousand."

"I guess ya know what yer doin', Will, givin' up worry fer hard work an' more worry."

"If I don't like farming in Teton Valley," said Will, "the Austins say they'll take me back."

"I had a friend who went up there way back in the nineties," said John. "Got a good farm and done good. He's dead now. We worked hammering nails and played together—sowed a few wild oats—won't tell you all the story, but a girl named Emma off a farm in Cache Valley was livin' in Ogden, Twenty-fifth Street—a chippy, a woman of the night. She fell in love with my friend and got him to marry her and take her to Teton Basin. My friend told me that on his farm Emma could work like a man—good as the best hired men. She was a prize, like my wife—I got what I asked for in her—well, them two cleared that land and got a good start when she up and died."

I listened. He was talking about people in my hometown. "Did you say his farm was in the south end of the valley?" I asked.

"Don't know whether I did or not—but it was," he said.

"Why was she a prostitute?" I asked.

"I saw you perkin' up there all ears," he said, "and now you ask questions—"

"Ya," I said, "what was your friend's name?"

"Curious as an owl," he said with a slight smile. "Better not tell ye that."

"What about Emma?" I said.

"I don't know," he answered. "I heard that her father had a farm, that his wife had died, that the girl worked with a lot of men . . . well . . . she was too big and not pretty, and these young men full of hell . . . well . . . I don't take no stock in chippies practicin' or reformed. But this one went straight, up there in Teton Basin, and after her death her husband got religious."

The next morning as we left, John said to Uncle Will, "Watch out for that inquisitive young man, and take care of the horses. Looks like you got some good horseflesh there."

As we went toward our destination, I kept thinking of the story of the prostitute and about my stepfather, who had died when I was eight. We still owned his farm, the one he and his wife cleared of trees and brush. After his wife died, he married my mother and became active in the church. His first wife's name was Emma.

OLD BUD

Every family in Victor owned one or two dogs. These dogs, like people, congregated at night to play, quarrel and spark. There were Great Danes that looked like Labradors, Airedales with long bodies and short legs like dachshunds, small sheepdogs with watery eyes like cocker spaniels, and greyhounds with bulldog faces—mongrels all. Every mongrel dog remained a dog and led a dog's life. I owned a dog, raised him from a pup, but I never slept with him, kissed him, or let him eat at my table.

At Lamoine Hatch's farm on a sunbright spring day I saw a mother dog nursing five cuddly puppies.

All were black with a white spot or two around the face except one, which was speckled black and white like a Dominique chicken.

"Give me that odd one," I asked Lamoine.

Teasing me, he answered, "That one is a son of a bitch."

"I know," I said, "there are three sons of a bitch there."

When weaning time came, I took my puppy home. "He looks like a pussy willow," Cora said. "Name him Bud."

I fixed up a bed for him out of two apple boxes, put it with him in it in the corner of the barn, and stayed with him until he went to sleep the first few nights. I petted him and played with him every day. How happily Bud would greet me each morning! How deeply he loved! Nobody, no living thing has ever showed me more genuine, unconditional, undying love than my dog Bud. He danced around me, barked with joy, and licked my hand with unadulterated devotion.

Bud and I grew up together. He grew muscular, powerful as a wolf. Proud of his powers, he frightened small and timid dogs away. Then he wandered at nights asserting his authority, proving his leadership with tooth and fang. Sometimes I found him in the morning beaten and bleeding from his nocturnal adventures. Once he pled with me in plaintive whines to relieve him from the pain of porcupine quills in his mouth, nose, and face. He patiently submitted to the operation as I pulled them out one by one, then he thrashed around in profuse dog courtesies of thanks.

I made a harness for Bud, hitched him to my sled, and taught him to pull. He became my Labrador, mushing through snow on beaten paths and roads. Then as I grew older my little brother seemed to inherit the delight of dog and sled, and with it a good measure of dog devotion. He sped with pleasure around town on the sled pulled by the big dog.

Then came the time when Bud grew old and feeble. He had weathered winters of ice and snow, suffered and recovered from wounds of battle, survived attacks of distemper, and now, limited in motion with arthritis, hampered in action with impaired hearing and dim sight, he lived both night and day in distress and pain. Stepfather Avery had joined the family now. We all decided in conference that Bud must be killed to relieve his suffering.

One morning when all the others were asleep Dad Avery got up, called Bud, who staggered on his stiff legs to follow, and with an axe in his hand went with the dog across the forty to a swale by the willows. Then he struck the faithful dog a death blow in the head and left the body there with the intent to return and bury it later. About an hour later Dad and I were in the corral when old invincible Bud, his head mashed and bleeding, came staggering up to Dad, whined, and licked his hand. Stepfather Avery was a man of fifty, a rancher, sheepman, and farmer who had trained wild horses to ride and work, branded and dehorned cattle, and slaughtered animals, all done with the detached emotion that such men must acquire, but at the sight of old Bud and his suffering I saw his wide-eyed look of horror.

I petted Bud. "What happened?" I asked. "By my word," Dad said in deep distress, "I killed him! I—left him for dead—not enough—harder to kill than a porcupine! I'll have to do it again."

Again he went off through the field with the axe in hand and the feeble dog following.

Who Would Tell?

One night after work on the farm my stepfather said to me, "Nice young man you met today—the one who came out in the field to see me—Isaac Wakely."

"I liked him," I said with only casual interest.

"There is a story in his life," he said. "His parents, my good friends in Emery County, Utah, planned to kill him when he was born."

"Your friends," I said, "planned to kill a baby?"

"Yes," he said.

"Good people?" I questioned.

"I'll tell you the true story," he said.

He sat on the plow seat, and I on the soft ground, as he began:

"This young man that you met is the oldest child of Mary and Edwin Wakely. These two fell in love—teenage infatuation—jumped over the traces, and she got pregnant."

"How old were they?" I asked.

"Young . . . in high school . . . seventeen or eighteen. They didn't tell their parents—afraid to—or didn't want to disappoint them. Both her parents and his were very religious—leaders in the church. Her father, the bishop, ran the local church. I knew their parents well. Her father—good man, but strict—made young fornicators stand up before the congregation in church and ask forgiveness."

"Oh, I see," I interrupted. "They decided to escape public condemnation by killing the baby after it came."

"It almost worked," he continued. "They succeeded in getting the parents to let them get married. Mary, the girl, had an uncle on a ranch down on Boulder Creek about 150 miles south, an isolated place. He wanted to retire, move off his place. He liked the boy, Edwin. The kid was dependable, ambitious, a farm boy with promising potential—almost your age, about like you."

"Not like me," I said. "I don't get in his kind of trouble and decide to kill a baby."

"They were good kids," he continued, "but they played with fire and got burned. If young people have good self-discipline and never balance on the edge of a cliff, they won't fall over."

"—and have a baby to kill," I added.

"These kids moved out on that ranch and stayed there—didn't mix with anyone until the baby came. Their nearest neighbor lived a half mile down the road. The rancher's wife who lived there took an interest in the young couple and tried to be friendly."

"Nosy?" I asked.

"Not exactly," he continued. "Rather a friend in their need. In early September the baby came to that inexperienced couple alone—no doctor, nurse, or attendant—and they, burdened with a plan to hide a sin with a greater one. A long night of moans and groans of the pains of labor from Mary rasped the heartstrings of Edwin, waiting, watching, worrying away hours before the birth. Nauseated and overwhelmed with the messiness of it all, Edwin left Mary in bed in tears, utterly exhausted, and carried the baby wrapped in a blanket out to the barn, laid it on hay in a manger, and sat on a rail beside it. He looked into the baby's face. A new feeling engulfed him. Here he saw the magic of new life, product of his own blood. He felt weak and helpless at the vision of the living child murdered and buried—the horror of it! He heard the sound of a vehicle outside."

"How do you know this story?" I interrupted.

"Years after this happened Edwin worked for me. We here friends. He told me about his folly."

"Go on with the story," I urged.

"Dazed, Edwin went out of the barn and there in a buggy sat the neighbor lady."

"Hello," she said. "What on earth troubles you, tears running down your face—white as ashes—limp as a dishrag?"

"Mary is sick," he said.

"Well, let's go in and take care of her," she said.

Facts of life and nuances of human behavior were not obscure to this lady. She saw what had been going on in the home and in Edwin and Mary.

"Where is the baby?" she asked.

Edwin stood as if stunned. Mary broke into a loud wail. Neither spoke.

"Come, come," she said. "Where is it?"

"It is—it is in the barn," Edwin said.

"Not dead?" said Mary. "Not dead!"

"Bring it in," she ordered. "We must clean it up. There is work to do."

This neighbor woman not only took care of the baby's immediate needs, but guided the young couple in mending their lives. She advised them to forget and never tell anyone about their foolish plan to kill the baby.

They named the boy Isaac because he was miraculously saved like Isaac, son of Abraham.

"What a story!" I commented.

"Yes," he said. "Edwin and Mary matured through this experience. They loved Isaac, gave him and their other children the good life."

"Does Isaac know the story?" I asked.

"Who would tell him?" he answered. "I suspect that no one knows how they planned to kill him except the parents, the neighbor lady, and me."

WORK HORSES AND MICE

The only threshing machine in the south end of the valley belonged to Big Dick Kearsley. It was modern, powered by a steam engine, a tractorlike miniature of a railroad locomotive. It pulled the thresher (called a separator, since it separated the grain from the straw and chaff) from farm to farm, then ran the thresher by means of a huge flywheel and a long, forty-foot belt. Dick's thresher far surpassed the old horse-powered ones in several ways: efficiency in getting all the grain from the straw, its automatic twine cutter, and a blower, to exhume the straw, replacing the old straw carrier.

The bumper crop of wheat, barley, and oats pleased the farmers. In early September, Dick Kearsley oiled up the thresher, fired up the boiler, put dressing on the six-inch, forty-foot belt, hitched horses to the water-and-coal wagon, and started threshing.

In preparation for threshing, farmers had cut the grain with binders that tied it with binder twine into forkfull-size bundles. Then they stacked the grain-laden bundles in round stacks wide as a silo and tall as a house.

Every morning at daybreak Dick and his assistant would fire up the boiler. The farmer furnished the men—two to pitch bundles, one to feed the separator, two to catch and transport the grain to the granary, and one to stack straw. Day after day the thresher puffed and rattled on from farm to farm completing the harvest.

More acreage of grain and higher yields overburdened the thresher. There were short delays, the usual ones of breakage and repair which Dick managed with expert efficiency. He could not, however, manage the great enemy of threshing: bad weather. Day after day storm clouds pushed relentlessly over Pine Creek Pass and opened the dump gates in the valley, halting threshing, and, as winter threatened, drove unthreshed farmers into panic. "Will I get threshed at all? Will winter weather drive even the iron horse into shelter?"

An icy December wind whipped down the canyon from the snowy mountains on the day the steam tractor pulling the thresher made its way up the road to our farm at the mouth of Pole Canyon to thresh our eight stacks of grain. At the farthest edge near the farmyard where the stacks stood, a small hill challenged the tractor, most of the weight of which lay at the big back wheels. Suddenly the front end rose in the air like a bucking rodeo horse. Quickly Dick released the power and the front dropped with a crash. Dick relaxed, smiled a little, and said, "The rearing bastard! He must have smelled a skunk!" Dick applied power carefully and slowly made the hill.

I never admired the gruff yet high-principled Dick Kearsley as much as I did that day. Toward the end of a long season of painful labor and harrowing frustrations, when I expected his heart, mind, and soul to be burned like his face and callused like his hands, he retained an unbeaten spirit and a sardonic wit that dispelled fright and despair.

The rich, black loam at our stackyard, now pillow soft with rain, furnished no footing for the big tractor, which ground itself deep into the mud. Dick detached it from the separator, pulled it away, and hitched his water-wagon team, big seventeen-hundred-pound workhorses, to the thresher to pull it into position. But with all the urging, with cusswords and whip, the big team could not move the machine.

"Will," Dick said, turning to my stepfather, "why, for Lord's sake, don't you put an acre of that rock patch on your other farm here so this straw eater won't sink down to hell in mud?"

Will laughed and said, "I'll pull it out with my team."

"With them mice?" Dick said. "In this muck they couldn't move a wheelbarrow."

The men all laughed.

"I'll try it!" Will said.

I trembled inside. That big machine looked frightfully formidable. The team referred to as mice were twelve-hundred-pound bays, Dove and Nell, beautifully matched. They were our multi-purpose team—the buggy team to run a mile or two, the cutter team to trot and ring the bells on Christmas, and the workhorses to pull the plow or binder in crop time. Now that heavy farm work was over, our other teams were retired to pasture and feedlot. We had deep devotion for Dove and Nell; we cared for them lovingly, fed them well, yet worked them hard, and they responded faithfully. I had noted how Dick's big team had not really put weight to the collar and I knew that Dove and Nell would; yet, I feared that Dad had put too much faith in our team. Here, I felt, stood a David against a Goliath.

Dad confidently brought out the little team, harnessed and ready, and attached the tugs to the doubletree while Dick stood by with an incredulous look of dismay and disbelief. I stood aside, tense—my heart pounding as if I were in a race. I wanted—I wanted so much for "them damn mice" to win. I felt as if I were a Ben Hur pitted against a Messala.

Dad tightened the reins, spoke softly, and the team stepped forward, tightened the tugs to feel the weight and place their feet for the pull. The men stood by in tense interest.

"Get up," said Dad in the sharp tone that always put the team in gear. At that moment I was glad he was driving instead of me, for I knew that he knew exactly how to hold the reins and how to speak to get the best possible performance from the team. I knew that as Dove and Nell pulled neither would let the other get ahead to force the other into disadvantage.

With more urging the team leaned forward and lowered their weight closer to the ground. Dove's right back leg slipped in the mud. In instantaneous timing Dad called, "Whoa."

The horses stood at rest.

"Up, up," Dad called with a slight movement of the reins. The horses placed feet again, and again Dad called, "Get up."

As the team strained so confidently to move this dead weight, I thought that neither horse, neither Dove nor Nell, had focused their sharp, big black eyes on the enormity of the thing they were trying to move, for they showed no intent to give up.

Dove slipped and fell back again. With the team at rest Dad said to the men, "Get some rocks from the creek bed over there, baseball size, to fill that mud hole at Dove's right hind foot. She needs a lock for that horseshoe."

Dad moved to Dove's head and stroked her lovingly as he awaited the next action. I moved over to Nell and touched her neck, mutely giving off powerful waves of encouragement.

Now, with the mud hole reinforced, Dove and Nell again braced in full power for the pull. They took the stance of those horses we see in paintings that show the power in every cell of every muscle. The big machine broke loose. Like a wrestler who suddenly feels an advantage, the ready team found new footholds to keep the load moving.

Shouts of joy, a roar of delight arose from the men.

"Well, I'll be damned," said Dick. "I will be damned!"

While the thresher shook wheat from the straw the next day, I paused at my job at the wheat spout to speak to Dick.

"Them mice, huh," I said.

"Ya," he said, "or ants that can carry seven times their weight. You are a reader—ain't there a story about a mouse that whipped a lion?"

CHAPTER
11

A Crooked Style and a Crooked Way, 1919–1922

CHARLIE SPENCER, SR.

N o one could forget Charlie, a man as inoffensive as a cool summer breeze. Picture a man of sixty dressed in bib overalls, a denim jumper to match, and a slouch hat, sitting on the spring seat of a rattletrap wagon, driving a mangy bay team, moving slowly along the country road. This is a memory I have of Charlie Spencer. He drove with a loose line, and the unreined horses, relaxed like the driver, walked with heads hanging low while Charlie whistled contentedly, not a melody, not a tune, but just a monotone whistle as rhythmic as breathing. As he came toward you, you always heard his whistle punctuated by the click of wagon wheels. Someone said, "Charlie, why don't you whistle a tune instead of that noise?"

"Well," said Charlie, "you know, that sound I make is as sweet to me as any music."

Charlie never talked fast, never shouted, never argued, never scolded. He took time to enjoy every breath he breathed. He loved the mountains, the soil, his family, his horses, his cows, his sheep, and everything and everybody. He carried marble candy in his pockets to give to little children, who like bees scented the nectar and came for it.

One day we saw Charlie's team standing at the doors of the C. M. Hatch Store warehouse loading supplies. I suspect that everyone including Charlie himself would think Charlie's team the least likely in all Idaho to run away, but they did. The wagon was not braked, the lines not tied to tether them. A dog, sauntering by the horses' heels, suddenly attacked by a bigger one with guttural growls, raised a ruckus that frightened the sleepy-headed horses. They jumped in fear, and the resulting noises they made frightened them more. As they turned the corner at the store, off went the spring seat and boxes of groceries, scattering cans, packages, and broken bags of beans and sugar helter-skelter in the street. A block down the street the runaways, dodging another vehicle, ran into a rock pile, tipped over the wagon, broke the reach, and left the wagon box and back wheels behind as they ran frantically on and on, racing madly. Charlie stood on the warehouse platform motionless, hat in hand, watching. As the team turned out of sight he said quietly, almost proudly, "Cain't they run!"

CHARLIE SPENCER, JR.

Charlie Spencer, Sr., named his first son after himself. Of course, the name was Charles, but everyone called both father and son Charlie. This father, like many, wanted to attain some kind of immortality through posterity. As young Charlie matured, no father could have been more pleased with the development of his namesake than father Spencer. He grew friendly, pleasant, just, and individualistic—all inherent characteristics of his father. For him peer pressure did not exist. He had no problem being himself. As democratic as Walt Whitman, he neither condemned the lowly nor glorified the proud. These characteristics boldly appeared in his school days.

In grade school Eliza Griffith was the ugly duckling. Her mother had died. Her father, burdened with three little girls to succor and support, neglected their needs. Eliza's uncombed and matted hair, her soiled and ragged clothes, and her perpetually wet upper lip inspired in other children a new name for her: "Snot Nose." She became a social outcast, a loner. However, at noon hour one day I saw Charlie Spencer helping Eliza do arithmetic, and someone later said to him, "Charlie, you and Snot Nose! You an'—"

"Ya," said Charlie, "helped her with fractions."

"Snuff, snuff, snuff," said someone.

"Didn't care," said Charlie, "gave her my 'snot rag' and she blew."

They couldn't tease Charlie. Criticism ran off him like marbles off a desk top.

May Day of 1913 dawned in glory. It pushed away the thaw and frost of winter and lit the fire of desire in the hearts of pupils in the sixth grade to drink in the sunshine. A gregarious, articulate boy, Darwin, spawned and publicized a plan to "play hooky," to leave school at recess, hike to the sunlit side of Mt. Pinochle, and there bask in the beauty of spring. The plan gained approval. We all left school at recess—all except the studious June Dubois and the iconoclastic Charlie Spencer.

Many years later, in high school, students signed a petition refusing to attend school unless a teacher, Miss Spurns, was dismissed. Only Charlie and one other of a student body of seventy-five refused to sign. The teacher was unjustly expelled.

One way Charlie differed from his father surfaced in a Farm Management class assignment. He platted an eighty-acre farm with house, barns, sheds, garden, pasture, and crop plots. I saw his plan with everything symmetrical and well-ordered. "That is not your farm," I said. "Your farm is crooked."

"This is my farm," Charlie answered. "Pa's farm is crooked."

"Why does he make everything crooked?" I asked.

"Well," he answered, "Pa says the stars are not straight in line, and they are pretty."

Sometimes Charlie made roses out of thorns, but like others he encountered thorns. The basketball coach drafted him to play on the team, not because he played fast or well, but because he stood taller than other boys, and that showed potential. He spent more time in play falling down and getting up than in running. One night, when he stood under the basket reaching to receive the ball, an opponent half his size struck his legs like a football tackle. Charlie's head and the ball bounced on the floor in unison. Charlie went out of the game and never returned.

The game ended before I learned that Charlie had not been injured, nor was he thrown out of the game by the coach. He had been called home where tragedy had struck. His father had died.

I never knew of the depth of Charlie's feelings at his father's death. As I knew him, he never cried, and rarely indeed did his smile break into a laugh. He respected and admired his father, that I knew. Such a youth as he, not yet possessor of a philosophic nor stoic mind, must feel the pain of darkness as well as the joy of light.

It must have been in his senior year shortly after his father's death that Charlie told me he was going to college. You are crazy, I thought. Poor farm boys like you and me can't go to college. I knew of only two boys of my acquaintance who had gone. They were sons of rich sheep ranchers, not boys whose fathers had died, like him and me.

"You are dreaming," I said. "It takes money."

"I'm going to the University of Idaho," he said, ignoring my comment.

That spring Charlie, Jr., at eighteen and with the guidance and approval of his mother, took over management of the farm. With good sense and ambition he mustered his younger brothers, Matthew and George, into service, awoke and reined up the sleepy-headed horses into action, plowed, planted, irrigated, and cultivated the land. The farm began to show signs of straight lines and at the same time to show beauty in its obdurate irregularity.

Crops flourished. The Spencer boys harvested an abundant crop. Charlie, Jr., boarded the train that fall bound for Moscow, Idaho, with money in his pocket for tuition at the university.

MATTHEW SPENCER

Matthew Spencer broke family tradition more than Charlie. The family rarely participated in public affairs—never attended church, parents and teachers meetings, dances, ball games, weddings, or funerals. Matthew, more gregarious than they, enjoyed a wider circle of friends than Charlie and developed a wit all his own. While he worked to supply family needs and to assist Charlie at school, he indulged his friendly nature in a moderate amount of recreation. He had been out of high school two years when Charlie graduated from college and got employment. Then Charlie helped support Matthew in college. At home, Matthew had made a joke of the irregularity of the Spencer farm as his father had established it, a joke in which the community participated. It was a mark of father Spencer's not easily erased—a trademark all his own. When he built his log home as he pioneered in the valley, he used no level, plumb, or square. He used no surveyor's skill, no road or landmark or north star to set it straight with anything. His eye never deceived him, for he never used it to set things on the square. No fence, nothing was square with Charlie's home. Then he built a barn ignoring plane geometry, a machine shed, a woodshed, a chicken coop, and even an outhouse, all cohesive only in their persistent diversity. His farmyard was truly a masterpiece of irregularity with no walls of any building parallel with any other building, or with any fence, or with any road.

At the University of Idaho Matthew studied animal husbandry. On a field trip, visiting farms and judging animals, his professor took the class to a farm that had been blown into disorder by a wind of tornado force. The barn had been lifted off its foundation and moved uneven with the house. The farm complex looked like a child's uneven drawing. Matthew got out of the bus, stood looking at the farmyard, and said, "God, this makes me homesick!"

WILLIAM SHADE AND SON

Farmer William Shade was the very antithesis of typical farmers of the day as city people saw them—men of the soil, at ease with themselves only in soiled clothes, men who could eat with their hats on, chew tobacco, curse their horses, wrestle calves, break broncos, and read nature better than they could read books.

Mr. Shade in dress, grooming, cleanliness, and manner of language appeared to be a gentleman farmer who loved the land and left the work to hired help. But Mr. Shade worked—worked hard on the farm even now when passing years were telling on him.

Three married sons were successfully established in professions and a fourth son, Noble, had just begun employment as a teacher. He had been and still was a challenge to a devoted mother and loving father. A hypertensive child, an intelligent, individualistic, iconoclastic adult, he showed potential for something—they hardly knew what. His innovative imagination led him to see life big and beautiful with nothing unattainable. Indeed, he saw everything big. He never really told lies; yet, if two dogs got into a fight and Noble saw it, his mind would visualize forty dogs on each side, each with alligator teeth and snake fangs.

His tastes leaned heavily toward the arts rather than to the mechanical or scientific. In childhood he could be Jack the Giant Killer, the wolf in "Little Red Riding Hood," or even Little Red Riding Hood herself. In high school he preferred *A Connecticut Yankee in King Arthur's Court* to *The Adventures of Huckleberry Finn*.

Early in childhood he showed originality in painting with crayons. He could draw a mountain in bold colors that resembled those of a bird and on it place a tree big as a forest and bright as a sunflower. Like William Blake he could see God in the tree and sketch Him there.

Before he went away to college he did an oil painting of his concept of "The Sacred Grove." It was chimeric and bright, a still-life that looked almost animated. His parents urged him to revise it—tame down the colors and brush out the fantastic. The result, approved by his parents after weeks of work, a rather surrealistic portrayal of a grove, he framed beautifully and presented to the church. There it gained sufficient approval of the Church Council to hang in the new church chapel.

Noble, however, remained a mystery. His mind induced the father to read Adler, James, and Freud on abnormal psychology, and to consult the wisest people—to meditate, to make a thorough case study of the boy and man—but all this he did to no avail.

Delos Lauritzen and the Bank Robber

Victor with its six hundred people prospered, prospered enough that the state of Idaho, with its liberal licensing of banks, allowed B. F. Blodgett and others to establish the Victor State Bank. Steve Meikle managed it; Delos Lauritzen assisted.

It was Saturday, Washington's birthday time. Some social affair in Driggs, eight miles to the north, had taken many Victor residents out of town, a break from the dark, dull days of winter. Business lagged in the sleepy town, especially at midday.

Delos alone kept the bank in the deserted town. Shortly after opening that day several customers came into the bank. Then hours passed without business. In the sleepy hour after lunch, a masked man entered the bank, walked in bold steps to the barred window, held a paper bag in one hand, leveled a gun at Delos, and said in a low, gruff voice, "Put all your money in this bag!"

Delos calmly deposited the money from the drawer into the bag.

"Walk slow back to the vault," demanded the gunman. The bandit followed around to the side door, opened it, and entered the inner office following the bank clerk.

"Go on to the vault," he ordered, "and unlock it."

Delos obeyed.

"Get inside," he demanded as he poked the six-shooter toward him in gesture. With Delos inside he shut the huge steel door and locked it.

The new bank, with the latest modern equipment, had a vault that could be unlocked from the inside, a fact of which, no doubt, the bandit was ignorant. Only seconds after the bandit left the bank with the money Delos came out of the vault, took a gun from a drawer, and hurriedly went outside to sight the escape of the thief. All was quiet; not a soul, man, woman or child, no horse nor automobile was in sight. The thief, Delos thought, must have transportation; a horse or a sleigh must be somewhere. He ran around the store to a side street. There stood a horse tied to a fence just beyond the store granary and warehouse where machinery was stored.

Delos knew that the money loss to the bank was negligible. The money drawer he emptied for the bandit contained only a small amount of cash. People en route to the celebration had stopped and withdrawn much of its supply. He felt relieved to know that he had not replenished it from the vault. But he wanted to catch the thief. He had a hunch that the man was in that warehouse removing his disguise. He did not hesitate in opening the warehouse door, nor did he take any precaution. In fact, he acted on instinct as if he were playing a game of cops and robbers as he had in childhood. He threw open the door. There indeed was the masked man with Levis dropped to his feet, revealing dress pants underneath. On a railing about six feet from him lay his gun. Hobbled by the Levis he was removing, the robber could not reach his gun before Delos had it. The banker overpowered him immediately and removed his mask. The thief was not an escaped convict, not a hardened criminal, not an experienced felon, but a well-known member of the community—a young schoolteacher of a one-room school in the north end of the valley, a man with his own meager account in the bank he robbed, and a member of a respected family, the Shades.

"You? You?" said Delos. "You a thief!"

"I . . . I just did it for fun," said Noble. "I planned on—"

"For fun—fun—you liar!" said Delos.

"You know . . . ," said Noble, trying to be nonchalant, "you know . . . I planned on . . . quick as I changed clothes . . ."

"You planned on . . ." said Delos.

"On bringing the money back," continued Noble, "just to show you how easy it is to scare you."

"You're a thief and a liar," said Delos.

"No, a joker, a Don Quixote. You . . . you know . . . it's . . . it's a prank," pleaded Noble. "I would return the money."

"I'll take the money back to the bank and you can tell that story to the sheriff."

He escorted Noble back to the bank, called the sheriff, and held the robber until he arrived.

The story of the bank robbery spread through the community like smallpox. To the people Delos was brave.

NOBLE SHADE

Noble, who perched precariously on the outer edge of reality, lived in the make-believe world of his creative imagination, and he preferred his world to the world of hard facts, of bone and brawn. Noble Shade, the dreamer, preferred swinging on a star to teetering on a willow tree. But earth life is made up of terra firma and demands feet on the ground and sweat on the brow. Now having become a man, Noble found imperative pressures to move out of fairyland. In attempts to yield, he planned grandiose schemes.

In Felt School District where he had begun teaching, he found a beautiful young lady. She was his Roselyn, his Juliet. He told her wonderful stories of a silver-lined future. He had a coal mine in the mountains to the west from which coal, mined by well-paid miners, would soon move on a conveyor belt to the railroad to be shipped to all the land. Teton Valley would prosper and he would be wealthy. Money to initiate the project was in the bank.

He had the love of the girl, but, denuded of the substance of his dreams, he feared he would lose her. In the heat of another flight of his creative mind he robbed the bank, got caught, and was locked in jail.

The rash act startled the community, alarmed the church, and threw his doting parents into devastating shock. Mr. Shade could not allow his poetic son, his innocent Adonis, to rot in prison. To save him he hired the best lawyers to defend him. As a result, after trial and deliberation a jury found

Noble "not guilty, by reason of insanity." They were convinced that his unlawful action was an irresponsible act of a mind victimized by schizo-phrenic tendency.

12

Colorful Communicators, 1910–1932

DARREL BRESSLER

F ive-year-old Darrel sparkled like a firecracker fuse. A handsome, bright, fearless child with confidence combined with a pleasing, lisping speech defect, he attracted attention. From his elders he had picked up a distinctive vocabulary incongruous with his tender age and innocence. Men and teenage boys, themselves schooled in approved speech, though shocked at hearing mountain-man expletives from a child's lips, gathered around and questioned him to hear his responses.

Darrel had been told he was cute, believed it, and responded to any audience by playing the part. In Darrel's case it appeared that there were no observers too pious, prudish, or sophisticated to laugh at his profanity, tempered somewhat as it was by his delightful lisp and obvious innocence.

One Saturday in winter Darrel appeared in Hatch's store. Soon becoming aware that he was being watched, he moved confidently among the teenagers around the potbellied stove. Imitating a big cowboy, he took a cigarette out of his pocket, put it in his mouth, lit it, sat down on a chair, put his feet on the brass warming rail circling the stove, and puffed on the cigarette. Older boys ogled him, amazed at his daring. He took the cigarette out of his mouth, blew out the smoke like a veteran smoker, looked at the boys, and said, "Hellth thake, ain't you guyth never theen anybody thmoke before?"

The Bressler family lived on a farm a half mile from the center of town across Trail Creek to the northeast near Ed McDonald's home. Ed especially enjoyed his young neighbor's sonorous outbreaks. One day, riding his horse across the flat toward town, Ed saw Darrel walking ahead of him. To overtake him and tease him and hear his rebuffs, Ed spurred his horse into a gallop. To escape being trampled, Darrel ran off the road into the sagebrush. Ed followed until Darrel tripped over brush and fell. Ed reined his horse. Darrel jumped up with a rock in each hand and, throwing back his arm like a baseball pitcher, yelled, "Now, God damn you, thurrender."

Ed said, "I was just trying to catch up to you. Do you want a ride?"

"Thure I do!" Darrel answered, dropping the rocks.

"Well, jump on behind me," said Ed.

Darrel looked up at the tall horse and said, "Jethuth Chrith, what do you think I am, a grathhopper?"

GEORGE MURDOCK

George had charisma. He talked fast, whipping out words with staccato finality and with an accent all his own. His speech provided a departure from humdrum communication. To the community George was the amusing Dogberrian, the master of malapropisms.

In early spring the watermaster called to George, "We are going to clean out the canal on Saturday. Will you come and help?"

George called back, "Ya, I'll tum myself or send a prostitute."

Albert Moulton met George one day and said, "Mornin', George, how ya doin'?"

"We're all o-tay at towr house, but Seed in plegnant and pig an don' feel well." The one called "Seed" was his sister, Theda, whose name had been contracted to Theed.

Albert asked, "How are your crops coming? Are you going to have a good harvest?"

"Mebby so, mebby not," answered George, "people been stealin' my watta—tant tro trops witout watta. I leave ma watta runnin' on ma lutern at night an det up at taylight an, by damn, ta watta taint got noplace. So at night wen it's ma turn, I set ma watta an go to ta teddate and hide, an, by damn, sure enough, dare tum ole Jack R., an in da dark I see dat battard open his teddate an' take ma watta. I knew it war Jack. I rectified him in the dark."

"What did you do?" asked Albert.

"I say to him, 'Ya want watta, do ya, Jack—I'll give it to ya,' an' I pickt tim up and trowed him into ta deep watta above da tedgates, an' he goes unde an' tums up spittin' an' beggin', 'Done trown me, George! Done trown me.' So I pusht tim unde again."

"For hell's sake!" said Albert with a slight smile.

"I let tim out," said George, "an' wile he stood dare weasin' an' shakin' I says, 'Now if ya ever steal ma watta again, I'll trow ya in an' keep ya unde till yar tungs bust.'"

"Jack a water thief!" said Albert.

"He was," said George, "he took my irritation watta, but he's resented, he won't steal watta anymore."

George Rust

Now, after over a half century since I knew him, I remember George Rust as a German immigrant of Aryan pride and as an Anglo-Saxon incarnate. When I was eighteen, George Rust owned and operated one of those fertile farms along the String. The dirt road that went up Pole Canyon separated his farm from ours. George Rust's farm produced the best crops of any farm in the area. Now about middle age, George had grown up on a farm in Germany and had been in America long enough to learn to communicate in English. He lived in a small log house on the farm with his brother Willie (pronounced Villie). I never heard Willie say anything in English except "damn it!" In planting time, in summer, and in harvest time George and Willie worked in the fields. In daylight whenever one looked at the Rust farm he could find George and Willie faithfully laboring. They worked like vassals chained to the farm. They never attended public gatherings, partied, traveled, or took vacations. They embodied the best tradition of German industry, integrity, and frugality. I think that George was so frightened of leisure time that he would do anything to get rid of it.

Immigrants who spoke a foreign language, who worked in America and learned English entirely by ear, often learned and used the crude and vulgar English. They seemed to be unaware of the stigma attached to certain words in polite society. George had learned English from common workmen. One spring day as Mother and I passed by in a buggy we saw, just inside George's fence in Warm Creek, masses of watercress. George stood near, we stopped, and Mother asked him if we could gather some cress. George acted especially glad to share. As we gathered it, we all heard splashing in the water and at once all three turned to see two toads copulating. George at once described the action with a thoroughly taboo Anglo-Saxon word. At that time I could hardly believe that any man would say it before a woman. I turned quickly and looked at Mother, wondering if she even knew the word. When I saw her face, I knew she knew and by her embarrassed, subdued smile I knew she recognized George's innocence and my awareness of his faux pas.

The winter of 1919–20 passed with but little snow and the following summer with little rain, resulting in drought and a shortage of water for irrigation. Crops failed, livestock suffered. To save animals through the winter, ranchers bought baled hay shipped in on the railroad at eight times its normal price. The weekly *Teton Valley News* reported that only three farmers in the valley had hay left when spring crops were planted—George Rust and two others.

One day I crossed the road from our farm to George's and in conversation said to George, "Why didn't you sell that stack of hay when you could have got forty dollars a ton?"

"I ain't had no chance to sell no hay," he answered. "People come to me and say, 'Sell me hay' and I say, 'You got any money?' and they say, 'No, I'll pay you next fall'—they beg me—and I say, 'No money, no hay,' and they go away mad and say, 'My cows are starving, and George Rust won't sell me no hay!—he's a son of a bitch.' Now suppose I give him hay on a promise, and fall comes, and I go to him and say, 'Pay me what you owe!' Then he will say, 'I ain't got no money, and that son-of-a-bitch George Rust is tryin' to make me pay.' So . . . you see," concluded George, "I just as well be the son of a bitch in the first place."

MISS RIPLINGER AND ORSON

Miss Riplinger sat at the desk in her third- and fourth-grade room hurriedly arranging materials for the first lesson. She must finish quickly, for school time was near. Usually she greeted students as they arrived, but not that day. She ignored the noise until pandemonium broke loose. A glance around revealed that Orson had again blown chalk dust into Eliza's face and with an eraser pounded dust into her hair. Pieces of chalk were crushed on the floor and pencil shavings from the sharpener scattered about. The teacher arose and exercised her pedagogic authority to establish order, and promptly set Orson to work cleaning up the mess.

The bell rang and the children, except Orson, took their seats. As Miss Riplinger began the lesson, Orson put the last eraser in place and moped to his seat, scrubbing his feet on the board floor as he walked.

Miss Riplinger loved all of her pupils, but she found it hardest to love hyperactive Orson, dull and dirty Eliza, and prudish Thelma. She felt relieved, now that Orson was in his seat behind Thelma. Then Thelma, the voluntary teacher's helper and guardian of the morals and behavior of all the class, held up her hand.

"Yes, Thelma," the teacher said.

"Miss Riplinger, Orson called you a son of a bitch."

Oh, Thelma, the teacher thought, why must you? Now I am obligated to deal with the tattletale report that everyone in the room knows.

Orson already looked guilty and cowered in his seat.

Miss Riplinger walked down the aisle and stood above him. He tried to squeeze under his desk.

"Orson," she said, "did you say I was . . . that?"

He raised himself up a bit, looked sheepishly at the teacher, and said, "Yes, Miss Riplinger, I did, but the minute I said you was, I said you wasn't."

WHISPERING ED

In our town lived many Kearsleys, several of whom were named Edward. Nicknames developed to distinguish them one from another. Thus we had "Whispering Ed," so named because he talked so loud. His vocal cords supplied natural amplification triple the decibels of those of other voices. He not only talked loud, he talked long. His wife talked, too; she talked loud to compete with Ed and fast to get the lead. His children, a half dozen of them, talked and yelled for obvious reasons.

I was in their home for dinner once. The pre-dinner conviviality sounded as spirited as six coyotes in a yapping contest. In the midst of the din, Ed's voice boomed above it all: "If you damn kids will shut your mouths, we'll have the blessin'."

They heard and responded—it was like the dramatic ending of a Stravinsky symphony. Then to my surprise Ed spoke to the Lord as if He were present.

Later I had another experience with this big-hearted, big-voiced man. He approached me one day where I worked on the farm. It happened this way. There was a horse, one that could jump a fence like an antelope, that liked the taste of the growing wheat on our farm. I ran him down and put him out time and time again until my patience ran out and my thoughts became profane. To scare him away I "tin-canned" him—put rocks in a large tin can, wired it to his tail with a leash long enough to let it bounce and rattle, and sent him running away. To my amusement the horse, frightened at the noise, bounded madly into the darkness.

The next day I learned that Whispering Ed had civil authority. "I got a paper for ye, Tommy," he said. "Ye done a damn foolish thing. Ye are arrested for cruelty to animals and endangerin' the lives of people."

I learned that Ed was Justice of the Peace and that my act would cost me seventeen dollars and a blot on my record.

About a dozen years later Ed had a serious attack of abdominal pain and vomiting. Dr. Redner came from Driggs, at the Kearsleys' request, examined him, and said, "I think you have appendicitis."

With a smile Whispering Ed boomed, "You damned old cuss, I've had this pain for fifteen years and you call it appendicitis."

"You better have an operation," the doctor said.

Ed refused to be operated on and became desperately ill. Soon the pain subsided and fever increased. Among many visitors who came to comfort him was the Reverend Mr. Shannon. This man, now old, had served his church and God long and faithfully in the Midwest. Now he lived with his son, the forest ranger, in Victor. His wife had died and without her and without the daily contacts with his former loving followers, he was a lonely man. Most of the settlers in the valley who professed any religion were from Utah and not of his faith. Being kindly and service-minded, however, he often visited the sick.

At Ed's bedside Shannon said, "Do you know the Lord Jesus Christ, how He can comfort you and forgive your sins?"

"You bet your life I know!" Ed shouted. "We know more about the Lord Jesus Christ and His power than you fellows will ever know."

The old man did not argue. He walked home taking the small steps of a feeble man, his stoic face bowed, his eyes focused on the ground.

Whispering Ed died of an infection from a burst appendix. The Reverend Mr. Shannon did not attend the funeral.

The Merchant, the Farmer, and I, 1912–1934

C. M. HATCH, THE MERCHANT

The sign, "B. F. Blodgett, General Merchandise," was painted on the wall above the door of the store. Benjamin Franklin Blodgett, the owner and operator, was the product of *Poor Richard's* philosophy, especially the parts about frugality: "A penny saved is a penny earned," and "God helps those who help themselves."

A servant of the people, Blodgett provided them with the necessities—for a price. From him they got flour, germade, frying pans, calico, gingham, overalls, coal oil, lamp chimneys, windowpanes, stovepipe, rope, baling wire, horse collars—everything, everything—for a price. Blodgett could barter with farmers, trappers, Indians, and outlaws, trade horses, and price his merchandise—all for a profit. He demanded respect.

Blodgett inspired honesty; he upheld it and enforced it. If he trusted a good-risk farmer to his summer's needs with a promise to pay in the fall, and the man couldn't pay in the fall, Blodgett would accept cattle, horses, or land in lieu of cash—for a profit. If the farmer failed to bargain or in any way proved obstinate, the sheriff would pay him a visit. Blodgett became the owner of land and cattle.

Blodgett would never let anyone starve. He would give a poor family cracked eggs, putrid butter, broken soda crackers seasoned with mouse tracks, and charge to their dubious accounts a small bottle of laudanum to ease their toothache.

Blodgett became happy. His store bulged with merchandise, his ranch expanded, his cattle multiplied, his bank account burgeoned. All the young men in town wanted to be like Blodgett.

An ambitious young man, Carlos Marion Hatch, worked for Blodgett in the general store. He learned fast from the master merchandiser. Through earnest labor he went up step by step as Blodgett grew old, first to sit at the desk behind the swinging gate to order supplies under Blodgett's watchful eye and then to count the money, pay the help, and manage the store. Then, about 1911, the time came when the store sign was changed to read, "C. M. Hatch, General Merchandise."

The Blodgett frugality became the business acumen of the new owner. Like Blodgett, Hatch acquired the knowledge of profits and losses, of assets and liabilities, and managed, through driving hard bargains, to keep the profit end up.

But C. M. Hatch's energies were not all spent in the store; his civic interests led to community leadership overreaching his interest in personal gain. He served the community through productive years as mayor, chairman of the school board, county commissioner, and Idaho state senator. He led in establishing the Victor High School, in attracting the Oregon Short Line Railroad to the valley, in keeping the trade route to Jackson, Wyoming, through Teton Valley, and in withdrawing the isolated valley from large Fremont County to establish self-government in Teton County.

He being a very busy man and I a fifteen-year-old boy, I felt a burst of pride when he put a hand on my shoulder and talked to me alone.

One day at church the speaker, Brother Wilson, told the story of Jonah and the whale. He said, "God is all-powerful. He can do anything! There is nothing he cannot do. The story of Jonah is an example of God's power. Three days Jonah lay in the very bowels of the whale without food, without air, yet God kept him alive. Now if that ain't a miracle, what is?"

I chanced to see and be greeted after church by C. M. Hatch that day. He was disturbed at what he had heard. "Let me tell you something," he said to me. "There are many interpretations of the Bible. Brother Wilson is a fundamentalist. He interprets everything literally. Some stories in the Bible are folk stories, from inexperienced folk, and their stories are in the Bible because they teach great lessons. The story of Jonah is the story of a man foolish enough to try to escape from the presence of God—and he could not! That is the message—not the supernatural survival of a man swimming for three days in the digestive juices in a whale's guts. These narrow interpretations of the Bible rob it of its power to lead and encourage people toward moral maturity."

A month or two later I went early to the store to do some family shopping. Marion, as we called him, was at his desk, behind the gate near the potbellied stove, dressed in a clean white shirt with black half-sleeves. Over the shirt he wore a vest with a watch chain draped from pocket to pocket. His handsome face and full head of hair, prematurely gray, made him look the part of a man of significance. No other customers were in the store. Clerks were busy stocking shelves. Marion opened the gate and said, "Come in. Sit down a minute. I want to congratulate you for the honor you received in school."

"Thank you," I said.

"You are a capable boy," he said. "Now is the time for you to learn that you have opportunities, in our great country, to become what you want to become. You are in the spring of life now. Do you know what happens to that water that springs out of the ground on your farm? It runs into Warm Creek and Warm Creek runs into Teton River, Teton River into the mighty Snake River, and Snake River into the powerful Columbia—each of these rivers blessing the people with life-sustaining nourishment. You are like the spring on your farm. You can grow big like the Columbia, and en route serve thousands of people as do the rivers."

He concluded by saying, "In our country boys born in log cabins can become great leaders."

I went home thinking about the spring and the rivers.

Streets in town were wide like those in Salt Lake City. The former owner of the store, Blodgett, had built a hitching post in the street in front of the store—a twenty-five-foot-long rail bolted to posts set in the ground. On business days customers tied horses, teams hitched to wagons and buggies, to the hitching post.

C. M. Hatch, not always the first by whom the new is tried, was the first to own an automobile in our town—a shiny new Buick sedan, the prettiest thing on wheels to grace our town.

One advance promotes another. Automobiles popped up like mushrooms. Buicks were the kings, Dodges the queens, Studebakers the bishops, and Model T Fords the pawns in the chess game of the new transportation rage. Almost overnight the hitching post in front of the store moved to a side street and a gasoline pump graced the street where the hitching post had been. Store clerks flexed muscles raising gasoline with a pump handle from the large underground tank to fill the cylindrical glass ten-gallon bowl high enough above for gasoline to flow naturally into the automobile tanks when the valve on the hose was opened. Lines on the bowl, like those on measuring cups, marked gallons.

Now, added to the general merchandise store stock of food, clothing, and hardware came not only gasoline but automobile oil, tire patching and boots, tire pressure gauges, hand air pumps, and reliners for Model T Ford brakes. Hatch's horse barn, now abandoned, was replaced by a garage next to his impressive sandstone home.

Free enterprise boomed. The valley awoke. The horseless carriages electrified the people and frightened the horses. The town livery barn and the harness shop became garages. When all this happened and I saw C. M. Hatch drive out on Sunday with his wife, Jean, and their three little girls in their Buick, I believed what he had said about the rivers and life and opportunities.

CHARLES LINDSMAN, THE DAIRYMAN

Naham Curtis had grown old and had turned management of his well-equipped, fertile farm and sheep ranch on the String Canal over to his son-in-law, Charles Lindsman. Naham Curtis had had sheep, two herds, four thousand of them. They pastured in summer on national forest range and were fed on the ranch in winter and lambed there in lambing sheds in the spring. Curtis had concluded his sheep business—harvested the last crop of wool, marketed the lambs for lamb chops, and sold the ewes for mutton. Lindsman promptly tore down the lambing sheds, much to Curtis's disappointment, and built a cow barn.

Charles Lindsman had long nourished a secret ambition, a goal to reach, a veritable obsession: "I'm going to have the best damn dairy herd in the state," he said. Now that he had the farm to produce the feed, he hitched his wagon to his star and away he went. He became a dairyman, not a cowboy but a dairyman, a 100 percent dairyman. His greatest friends of humankind were the University of Idaho animal husbandry extension service men. He got the books and pamphlets they provided on dairying and followed instructions. If any suggested practice they proposed failed to work, Lindsman asked more questions and made a new start.

Lindsman took no interest in social life or sports and but little more in political or civic affairs, and his only thoughts on religion or immortality had to be in some way related to the eternality of the cow.

Lindsman reached his goal. He reached it, first of all, by getting a bull, a worthy sire with a pedigree (equal to the longest biblical "begats") showing the highest-producing dams for generations. This bull, King Schleswig Friesan Slott III, he bred to a cow of but little less royal blood (a cow he had bought as a calf) named Princess Schleswig Pearl IV, and in fifteen years he had a herd of twenty-five pedigreed Pearl-Slott Holsteins unmatched for milk production in the state of Idaho. How did Charles Lindsman do it? He did it by choosing heredity and by providing the best possible environment for milk-producing cows.

Even a casual acquaintance of Charles Lindsman could not help but be impressed with his tender devotion to his cows. He knew the pedigree name of each cow, the date of birth, number of offspring, date of birth of her last calf, date bred, period of lactation, pounds of milk production per day with its percent of butterfat. He knew the habits and characteristics of each cow. He also knew the records of the best-producing dairy cows in the country. In short he knew the dairy business from A to Z. The Lindsman dairy stock was in demand in America.

Charles had a wife, Mable, and two young sons. Mable slaved at the kitchen stove, at the sink, in the washroom, in the garden. Occupation, avocation, recreation—everything on the Lindsman farm was work. At first Mable shared Charles's interest in building the dairy. But she observed that as he accomplished his purpose and as he collected blue ribbons of success, his eye became more and more focused on the glory of the cow, all to the neglect of things of the spirit. She maintained, quite accurately, that her husband's supply of admiration and affection was spent on his beloved Holsteins.

In the spring while Charles played midwife to freshening cows and gloried in the new crop of blooded bull and heifer calves, Mable went to Rexburg and gave birth to her third son. The pregnancy had not been easy. For months she had fought false labor pains and threatened miscarriage. The baby came, however, fully developed and lovable. It especially touched the lonely mother's heart. Mable returned home to resume her strenuous life. Soon she became overburdened with despondency. Then came the cruelest cut of fate: the baby suddenly died. Her husband, Charles, shared in the sorrow, but remained unaware of the depth of Mable's emotion. He did not mean to be unkind, but only to be motivated by practicality and reason. He said, "We will not go to Rexburg to buy a casket. We will not have a funeral. I will bury the body on the farm."

"No! Oh, no!" she said. "You will not treat our baby like a dead calf."

She left—went to her room to cry. Drained and dazed, she sat staring at her dead child. Deep into the night she sat there until, exhausted, she lay down and slept.

When she awoke the next morning, the baby was gone. She ran out to the barn where the men were milking. "You have taken the baby!" she cried.

"Yes," her husband said. "It is best, easiest for you. I buried it."

Mable could not speak. Rage, grief, sorrow, despair overwhelmed her. In nights to come, sleep, chief healer when the heart has bled, came only sporadically. Insomnia weakened her body and strengthened her resolution. The day came when she could confront her husband.

"I am leaving you, Charles," she said.

"Why?" he asked quite innocently.

"You ask me why? Have you no eyes to see, no sense of feeling? I am leaving you because I have failed as a wife and have become a chattel, a cow, if you please, or more than a cow, an ox, a cow to feed your appetites and an ox to pull the load. You milked your cows, took their butterfat and their off-spring. You milked me of my free will and took my baby. Why am I leaving you? Because my dead son speaks from the hell-hole where you buried him to tell me I have been a fool."

PEDAGOGY AND PANIC

Merchandising was not unknown to me, for I worked part time in a grocery store while attending school. Never did I think of storekeeping for a lifetime occupation. Dairy farming I knew, having worked on the farm, and I found it more inviting.

As a child I loved the out-of-doors—the sky and all the earth. On the farm I loved the animals—the lively horse, the motherly cow, the gentle lamb, the spirited calf, the furry cat, the faithful dog.

There were joys in many smells, sights, and sounds as one worked next to nature, such as the smell of new-mown hay, the sight of tiny rows of green wheat decorating the black earth, the sound of a gentle breeze in a field of ripening wheat.

But the farm of the 1920s demanded drudgery. Ours was a dairy farm that demanded not only day labor, but daily, unending, morning and evening milking and labor. A person must be a robot to take it. Contented farmers often praised the farm life with clichés such as "On the farm you are free," and "Here, you are your own boss. You don't have to take gaff from anyone." Rationalization these! A farmer is a slave to his animals and plants. Farmers who are free are farmers who fail.

The farm of that day required agonizing dirty work, branding, dehorning, castrating, and slaughtering animals. Pigpens, barns, and chicken coops had to be cleaned—scooped out. All this I abhorred.

At that time in Idaho one could qualify for the first year of teaching in one summer after high school. Much to the disappointment of my home folks, who had offered me liberal incentives to operate and acquire the fertile Durney farm, I took the shortcut to the teaching profession. I took the eight state-administered-and-scored exams to qualify for entrance to Teacher's College. I enjoyed the challenge, found it invigorating, daring, and hard, like climbing the rocky Tetons. This accomplished, I borrowed fifty dollars from Aunt Mary and went to summer school.

That autumn I returned to the schoolroom where I had sat a few years before, a pupil under the rule of Mrs. Cluff. Now I was the schoolmaster of the sixth grade. My students were my brother Gordon, six second cousins, and about twenty others. I entered the profession with less than an hour of practice teaching, a slight introduction to pedagogy. That year I became somewhat of a sergeant, a disciplinarian robbing both my students and myself of some of the joy of learning. Yet, by year's end, I had chosen teaching as my lifetime profession.

That summer I left my home country. After six years of study, teaching, and other adventures including marriage to Fern Allred of Paris, Idaho, I moved with her to Utah to complete study for an A.B. degree.

It was autumn 1929. Fern and I, both teachers, had worked together for two years and had saved enough to finance our needs for a year.

About a month before the birth of our first child that year, financial woes struck our country, beginning in October with the dramatic stock market crash, wiping out billions of dollars in paper profits of investors, bankrupting businessmen, closing banks, factories, and stores, and creating widespread unemployment.

In February I went to the Student Placement Office of the university to enroll for employment in high school English teaching.

"Prospects for employment in teaching are not good," said the director. "People are not able to pay their property taxes. The schools will suffer. Teachers will be released."

At home we looked into the future with apprehension to July, when our coffer would be empty. A few weeks passed, Fern feeding, cleaning, and rocking the baby while I worked with an overload of study to complete my final quarter for the degree.

Then came a burst of relief. Without application my home folk remembered me with an offer of employment: superintendent of schools. This title that sounds so lofty consisted of management of a twelve-teacher system of both grade and high schools.

That autumn of 1930 I returned to Victor at a salary a third higher than I had received before, two thousand dollars per year. Hard times had not yet struck Teton Basin with their fury. At the close of the year we teachers received contracts at the same salary for the coming school year.

Crops were good. When autumn came, pantries, root cellars, granaries, barns bulged with produce. For this and for cattle, sheep, and pigs sales were minimal. Farmers could not get money to buy clothes and pay taxes.

Schools were in financial distress. After our first month or two of school, we received pay in "warrants," a guarantee to pay face value plus 7 percent interest at some future date. I was making monthly car payments to a General Motors Acceptance Corporation office in the lower country. I wrote and asked them to accept a warrant for pay. They refused. My account became delinquent. I could have cashed my warrants at a bank at a 10 percent discount, but this usury irked me, and I refused. My creditors wrote and said they would repossess my car.

We were snowed in. In those days of no paved roads in the valley and no snow removal, we stored our cars for the winter at the first big snowfall, usually in December. Amused at their threat to repossess the car and feeling a bit Mephistophelean, I wrote, "Come and get it."

By the time the snow melted in May, I found sale for my warrants at par and paid my debt.

At the close of school in the spring of 1932, Idaho schools were in distress. The worried school board of my district refused to issue contracts to teachers for the next year. It left me and my teachers suspended—no place to go, for all Idaho teachers rode on the same sinking ship.

A few weeks before school opening time that year, they granted us contracts at half our previous year's salary. We all accepted the lifeboat to save us.

The meager pay for the 1931–32 year came in cash. Half salary supported us, for the cost of most necessities had fallen.

In the presidential election year of 1932 the distressed electorate ousted President Hoover and elected Franklin Delano Roosevelt. No president has ever acted more decisively and more rapidly to relieve the suffering of the needy than he. The Democratic legislature and their president united to establish work programs for about eleven million unemployed and needy people. The programs most beneficial for our area were the Civil Works Administration (CWA), later called the Works Progress Administration (WPA), and the Civilian Conservation Corps (CCC).

Now, in the third year of my tenure, 1932–33, my salary and the salaries of my teachers were restored to the first-year level. Federal government and local action had made it possible.

But that year was not roses for the farmers. The prices of farm products were horribly depressed. Howard Tanks observed that it would take twenty-five bushels of wheat to buy a doll that his little girl had requested from Santa for her Christmas.

Often that winter I looked down from my comfortable quarters on the second floor of the sandstone schoolhouse at about twenty men sawing wood by hand, wearing overshoes, mittens, and earmuffs against the wintry winds. Employed by the CWA government program, they pushed and pulled the six-foot saws across the logs to wear them away, while power buzz saws that could do the work of many men lay idle. Ambitious men worked as well as the lazy. As one of the latter, Glen Loafer could have been down there, for in that day the law of "root, hog, or die" operated inexorably.

As I came out of the school one night I met my friend of many years, Eldon Johnson, now a successful farmer, who pulled in toward the woodpile with his big team and bobsled loaded with logs.

"Eldon," I called, "must you work at logging in this wintry weather?"

"Got to buy shoes for my children," he answered.

These men I knew were being paid one dollar a day. Possibly Eldon got extra pay for his team. I, one of the beneficiaries of their toil, received $5.50 for every day of the year. These men, I thought, are serving the world better than I. They are providing survival necessities. They are providing fuel to heat the school building.

One cold day after school had closed, students had gone home, and the noise of industry and gaiety of crowds had ceased, I sat at my desk enjoying the silence. As darkness approached, I heard soft sounds coming from the men working at the woodpile. I arose from my chair and looked out the window. From my vantage point they were huge black ants, industrious as if they had been disturbed in their anthill. These are truly ants, I thought, in the same inverted anthill as I, each of us with his own assignment.

After that year I left my valley, taking with me a legacy of memories.

CHAPTER 14

Resters and Lawbreakers, 1898–1950

BILL BAUM, THE BARTENDER

A frontier town without a saloon is like a cowboy without spurs. It doesn't have the force to make it lively. Such a town attracts and breeds mountain men, and mountain men often feel the need for refreshment. Bill Baum established a saloon in Victor to supply and promote the need. His establishment was a room as long as a lasso rope and wide enough for a bar just a little longer than a wagon box. Whiskey freighted into the valley cost money, and money, scarce as hen's teeth, did not come fast nor easy enough to satisfy the thirst of some saloon patrons. Bill Baum posted a sign above a shelf of bottles behind the bar reading, "No money, no drink."

This saloonkeeper, like most of them, had a friendly smile, a strong will, and fast reaction time. He ran his business his way, with snap judgments and finality.

With holiday spirit, the bartender at Christmastime treated a house full of customers to a drink. Then when some of them refilled their glass over and over he arranged for ways to get the helpless home.

Two days after Christmas that year of 1898 a tragedy occurred at the saloon. In wintertime Baum's place with its warm fire became a convivial gathering place which, though promoted by the proprietor, was not profitable. At this time of year few of the traveling drinkers going and coming from Jackson's Hole were in town. Several local men warmed hands and feet at the stove in the saloon that night. Fred Sinclair drank at the bar. A homesteader thirty-four years old and unencumbered with wife or children, he found company and comfort at the saloon. Fred ran out of money and said to the bartender, "Give me another drink and charge it."

Pointing to the sign, the bartender said, "Can't ye read? No money, no drink."

"I live here. I'll pay!" Fred said. "Give me a chaser."

"I don't trust nobody, see? Anyway, ya've had enough!" said Baum.

"You know, Bill, I gotta have a drink," Fred begged.

"Shut your damn mouth or I'll throw you out," Bill said in anger.

Fred got up, slowly mumbling as he walked around behind the bar, "I'll get my own drink."

"Get out." Bill yelled. "Get the hell out of here!" As Fred continued to move in, Bill grabbed the nearest club, a full bottle, and with fire in his eyes swung at Fred's head. It struck squarely at the temple and Fred fell to the floor.

Startled, looking at the man lying on the floor, Bill said, "Better call Doc."

The man referred to as Doc was Doctor Woodburn, who had announced his name and title a short time before when he arrived in town. He established no office, displayed no diploma, and showed no professional manner. Most residents felt that only the gullible believed his claim of professionalism.

This doctor, when summoned to the saloon, pronounced Sinclair dead, a fact now evident. Then, assuming the coroner's role, he took the body to a cabin and performed an autopsy, as he said, to determine if the man died of the blow on the head or of acute alcoholism. Then authoritatively he said that the man was killed by a blow on the head.

Bill Baum, charged with murder and then taken to trial, had no lawyer to defend him. He pled his own case. "I didn't mean to kill him," he said. "I didn't—I just hit him to . . . to turn him . . . to keep him from taking my property."

"Did you hit him on the head with a bottle?" said the judge.

"Yes, but—"

"Did he die?"

"I didn't know," Bill said, "I didn't—he died too easy. He had no right to take my liquor."

Bill Baum's trial ended with his conviction for manslaughter and a short sentence in the Idaho state prison. He never returned to the valley.

DAVID PIERCE, THE POSTMASTER

Teenage boys in our frontier town had eyes open for fun. Halloween pranks such as ticktacking windows, loading or unloading wagons with wood or any available freight, tipping over outhouses, often carried over into other times and actions. One such adventure provided and dramatized evidence to condemn certain people.

Youth often wore away long winter nights by coming to town in a sleigh or on a saddle horse to paint the town. Law enforcement officers gave no heed to any lawlessness that appeared short of horse stealing or murder. In fact, few if any youth knew the county sheriff or the town constable. People looked on pranks as youthful expenditure of energy in wild-oat sowing that would not ruin the harvest—hence, pranks and rowdiness were irritations to be tolerated.

A favorite winter sport of cutting shines in the wide main street amused the shiners. When snow became packed down to icy solidity, a driver with a two-horse team hitched to a bobsleigh would gallop down the street with a load of young folk, then turn sharply to send the front and back runners of the sleigh swinging in a circle, the riders breaking the air with shouts of excitement.

Late one night, after George Smith tired his team with this activity, he tied his horses to the hitching post and with his pals went into the pool hall where they loitered until midnight. When they came out they saw something that merited investigation.

"Ain't that David P. crossin' the street down there by the post office?" said Jim.

"Looks like him," said Fred.

"Shut up and keep still," said George. "It's him all right. I'll sneak past the livery stable an' see if he goes into the hotel." Already out of the sleigh, he walked away carefully, keeping in the shadows.

At this time the two-story frame hotel had about eight bedrooms upstairs. It stood across the street from the post office and near the livery stable. Customers for the most part were travelers going to and from Jackson's Hole. A steady roomer there at this time, however, was a vivacious farm girl, Lucille, living in town and working as assistant to the postmaster.

George knew that the postmaster had sent his pregnant wife, Laura, away to her mother's to prepare clothes for the expected baby. His walking at midnight across the street toward the hotel was, therefore, an item inviting research.

"I'll be damned. I will be damned," George said as he returned to the sleigh, "that pious cuss is in Lucille's room."

"How do you know?" said Arlo.

"I followed him," said George. "The only light burnin' was in the lobby. He went upstairs, an' I snuck up an' saw—"

"The hell you say," interrupted Arlo.

"A door opened down the hall," continued George. "The light hit out at me, but I saw a skirt in the door to let him in."

"Wow," said Jim, "that heifer must a been—"

"Let's fool the bugger," said Fred. "Go and block the door of his house so he can't get in when he goes home."

"Listen," said George, "I got a idee. Them doors in the hotel hall is square across from each other. Let's wire them in."

"How? How can ya?" Arlo asked.

"Knob to knob across the hall. It's easy. They can't get out from either room."

They all laughed. "What if we get caught?" asked Fred.

"Somebody might come," said Arlo.

George's voice silenced the others. "It's like this—everybody 'cept Dave and Lucille is asleep. It's so quiet up there we can hear the bed squeak—an' them that squeak it won't kitch us."

A half hour later all four went to the hotel. Arlo guarded outside, Fred watched in the lobby, Jim guarded the hall. George, carrying the baling wire, in which he had fashioned a loop to put over a doorknob, slipped quietly as a cat down the hallway, listening for sounds in the rooms. He pushed the wire loop over the knob of the door across from Lucille's room, twisted it tight with pliers, cautiously avoiding a rattle that might awaken the occupant of the room. He listened for sounds in Lucille's room. No sound—nothing.

Someone coughed in an adjoining room. Startled, George held his breath. Hurriedly he wrapped the wire around the knob of Lucille's door, tightened it, and twisted it to tight tension between the two doors. He tip-toed down the hall. Outside in the winter air, with the tenseness of the adventure over, the pranksters relaxed. They were ready for the comfort of home and bed; yet they wanted to see the action when someone cut the wire to release the prisoners.

George yearned like a town gossip to reveal the perfidy of the respected postmaster and the flirtatious girl, but to do so would expose his own involvement.

The first word of this affair to hit the winds of gossip in town were those accusing David and Lucille of spending the night together. That news spread like wildfire, for no news, be it of disaster, or horror, or of reaching the pot of gold at the end of the rainbow, spreads in a small town like scandal.

This was doubly electrifying since the man accused of adultery had sown no wild oats, had served for two years as a missionary in France, attended church regularly, kept the word, and faithfully performed his priesthood duties as superintendent of the Sunday School. Furthermore, he was the respected postmaster.

This matter concerned the church. Interviewed by the bishop, Naham Curtis, David explained: "It was month's end report time. I went to Lucille's room with records to work with her to complete the accounting."

"But Ben Jones says you stayed all night," said Naham.

"Someone," said David, "locked us in. I couldn't get out until Ben unwired the door. Ben will tell you that."

"Why, David, did you stay all night locked in?"

"It was late, people were asleep. We didn't want to disturb them," explained David. "We did nothing wrong. I promise."

David continued his duties in the Sunday School. Since he was exonerated by the bishop, many residents of the community were ready, even eager, to exonerate him. They cited his moral leadership and clean record. Others of a different mold refused to believe in the innocence of the couple and took delight in the evidence of a sin committed that would strip one they called pious of his robes of righteousness.

As sunrise followed sunrise, whisperings diminished. Laura, David's wife, returned home, and home life returned to normal. The mail wagon came and went from "out below." Lucille sold stamps and delivered mail through the barred window to the customers, and canceled stamps on outgoing mail. David helped load and unload the mail wagon, sorted mail, kept the books, and ordered supplies.

Sunday School attendance increased. It appeared that curiosity led people there to watch and listen to see or hear if they could find in David any sign, visible or invisible, of his wearing a scarlet letter "A."

Time is a river of passing events with swift currents. One event soon passes on and another takes its place.

As lazy days of summer passed into hazy days of fall, Lucille, the postal clerk, left her post and stayed at hone. Then at the time of the first snowfall she was delivered of a baby boy. The timing of the event turned evidence into truth: David Pierce was the father of the child.

Aunt Mary came across the street one day eager to tell Mother the news. "They excommunicated Pierce today," she said.

"How do you know?" asked Mother.

"Asa heard it in town."

"It's a shame," said Mother, "a horrible shame that he did it."

"He is a good man," said Auntie. "Men are . . . well . . ."

"He'll repent—come back in the church," said Mother.

"I must hurry home," said Auntie, "—just thought you'd like to know." She lifted up her apron and hurried toward home.

Within the next month, Victor had a new postmaster. David Pierce and his wife with their two little children left the valley never to return.

GLEN LOAFER

On any clear summer day we could find Glen Loafer standing in the shade, leaning against the front wall of Ben Kearsley's barber shop, chewing gum. His hands would be in his pockets unless he had to blow his nose or scratch. He always chewed the gum slowly, the way a contented cow chews her cud. Only once did I see him accelerate the speed of his chewing. That happened when lightning struck a telephone pole a half block away and thunder blasted his eardrums.

Summer lightning storms meant tragedy to Glen. Only a year or two before when his mother, Maggie, was milking their cow, lightning struck and killed the cow and left her disabled.

Now both of Glen's parents were dead, and their three sons—William, twenty-one, Glen, twenty, and Theodore, sixteen—lived in the big house. William had a job, section hand on the railroad, and supported himself and his brothers. Glen did not work. He did not keep house; he kept away from the house. Nothing in Victor looked more lonely than the Loafer house except the haunted house northeast of the schoolhouse, and nothing in town looked more like the haunted house than it—it looked so lonely! The fence around it, which his father had built, now leaned and lopped without any utility except its inspiration to Glen, its natural relaxed and picturesque droopiness. The two-story frame house, no less distinctive than the fence, never having been painted, stood grey and wrinkled with wet and cold of winter snows and heat and rain of summer days. Some small panes in larger windows were out and the holes stuffed with faded pillows. Here and there torn or shattered remnants of green blinds showed through windows. The old house stood there uncared for, a fetish by day and a specter by night, while Glen chewed gum and rested.

Glen never buttoned his shirt sleeves in the mornings because he knew that if he did he would have to unbutton them at night. If his hand got too warm and sweaty in his pocket and he took it out and the pocket came with it, he never bothered to tuck the pocket back in.

More must be said about Glen's gum chewing. He chewed it constantly, skillfully, and frugally. He made one chew last three days. However, since his chin had grown long and his mouth big, he needed two and one-half sticks for one chew. Therefore, you can see that chewing gum gave him considerable exercise. Sometimes he would get tired and go to sleep. He could sleep standing up as well as any horse—that is, when he was leaning against a wall. The way you could tell that he was asleep was that he wouldn't be chewing. A stranger came by one day when he was asleep, took him for a scarecrow, pulled off his straw hat, and nearly toppled him over.

In those days before I left the valley, I felt sorry that Glen had not been born in a log cabin. A boy born in a log cabin could become president of the United States. Glen, born in the big frame house, didn't have a chance.

I have never seen any news in the papers about Glen Loafer since he made his last stand by Ben Kearsley's barber shop. No doubt he has just rusted out.

ALBERT AND HIS SWILL BARREL

I loathe swill barrels. I adore the thought of never seeing or smelling one again. A swill barrel is a potbellied, forty-gallon, wooden barrel for swill. Swill is a thick, soupy by-product of the farm home. Into the swill barrel of the farm home of seventy years ago went anything that had a calorie of food value. The basic ingredient was skim milk and whey. To this was added kitchen waste. The housewife would rinse dishes with a minimum amount of water and pour it into the swill along with potato and fruit peelings and any food without bone that once had been good but had aged and spoiled too much for human consumption. Open and exposed to hot sun, the barrel and its contents produced a brand of bacteria that processed skim milk, whey, garbage, and dishwater to make it swill, a fetid, foamy fluid that insults the olfactory nerves and can only be described by the word "pee-uh." A swill barrel has a smell akin to that of a decaying dead animal, a skunk, a fish cannery, and scalded feathered chickens. The only smell worse is the pig and the pigpen where swill is consumed.

We had a swill barrel; we kept it out behind the granary where wind carried its odor toward the pigpen. We "slopped" the pigs, a daily chore, with this hogwash. To me the word "swill" was the nastiest five-letter word in the English language. It is one up on those four-letter Anglo-Saxon vulgarisms. Only a pig (with all the connotations of the word "pig") could like swill, and I never heard of a pig getting sick on it. Pour a bucketful of this pig delicacy into the trough and pigs fight and squeal over it like a pack of hungry dogs with one piece of meat.

Whenever I think of swill barrels, I think of Albert. I knew him only slightly and have forgotten the errand that took me to his farm. I went there on a footpath through a broken gate to the front door and found it abandoned and blocked by cast-off furniture on the porch. I went to the back of the house. There I found a screened porch with a bashed-in screen door, and by the screen a putrid, pungent swill barrel. A red hen sat on the edge of the barrel selecting dainties from the swill at the top of the barrel. As I approached, the hen gracefully departed, leaving me with the swill and the flies, for flies are drawn to swill as iron filings are to a magnet. I shut my mouth in a vise-like grip, waved my hand before my face to protect my eyes, and, holding my breath, darted to the screen door. It resisted my entrance and I was bombarded with flies and bees, and asphyxiated and contaminated with the odor of swill. Gasping, I crossed the porch and gained access to the back door of the house.

Albert's buxom wife answered and informed me that I could likely find Albert asleep on the hay in the barn.

Asleep, I thought. A man in his prime asleep in the daytime, now in harvest time. "Is he sick?" I asked.

"No," she said, "just takin' it easy."

Chickens ran out of my way as I went through grass and weeds to the barnyard. Out of the trees I saw the barn leaning like the tower of Pisa, part of the roof broken down, and side boards broken off. I passed a woodpile where axe, saw, and chips were obviously lying where they had fallen. I stepped over a slop pail on the ground and wound through a barnyard of confusion—among other things a broken wagon, a barrow, a cast-off horse collar with padding coming out, broken harness straps, a pile of cans, a broken pig trough, and a one-legged milk stool. I reached the barn, climbed into the loft, successfully lifting myself past a broken ladder rung. There lay Albert asleep on the hay. I was impressed with his enormous girth, a swill-barrel girth.

I thought as I saw him there, so contentedly relaxed, that were I he, I too would yield to the urge to escape from the sights of overwhelming needful work and the detestable stink of swill to seek ambrosia in the inviting aroma of alfalfa hay.

CLYDE JAMES, THE BOOTLEGGER

The years 1920 to 1933 were known as the dry years in the United States, not because of a dearth of rainfall, but because of a dearth of "booze." This fact led to an acceleration in the birthrate of bootleggers—not of the old-time ones who smuggled flat flasks in their boots, but a new type of illegal producers and distributors of intoxicating liquor. Clyde James gained the title of Teton Basin Bootlegger.

Before 1920 temperance societies had sprung up throughout America and zealots for abstention from the use of liquor launched fiery campaigns. This was the time when sentimental folk sang the songs, "Oh, Touch Not the Wine Cup" and "Have Courage, My Boy, to Say 'No.'" This fervor resulted in the enactment of the Eighteenth Amendment to the Constitution of the United States, adopted in January 1919, which forbade "the manufacture, sale, or transportation of intoxicating liquors . . . for beverage purposes." A year later the Volstead Act provided for enforcement of the amendment, and Prohibition went into effect. Shortly illegal drinking places—"Speakeasies"— arose in cities, and small distilleries, lodged in hideouts in backwoods country, produced cheap liquor called by such colorful names as "still swill," "valley dry," "rotgut," and "mountain dew." Clyde James established a still in Trail

Creek Canyon. His business had much in common with that of Uncle Bill's still described in the folk song "Mountain Dew," which begins:

There's an old hollow tree down the road here from me
Where you lay down a dollar or two,
Then you go round the bend and you come back again
With the good old mountain dew.

Clyde grew up in the Teton Mountains in Idaho east of Victor, near the Wyoming line where his father owned and operated a small sawmill. A child of the woods, he knew the fir, pine, spruce, balsam, and "quaken asp" (he never knew them as aspens). He tramped on pine grass, ate chokecherries, serviceberries, and huckleberries, picked wild roses, larkspur, Indian heads, and sunflowers, heard wolves howl and coyotes bark, and awoke mornings to the cheerful call of the meadowlark or the sad notes of the mourning dove. He knew the feel of nature, but little of books and creeds. From the time he had strength enough to push the sawdust away from the buzz saw, he worked in the sawmill. As he grew up his father, his brother, and he chopped down the Douglas fir and white pine trees, lugged them with horses from the northern slopes of the mountains to the mill, and tore them into rough lumber with the big buzz saw.

When I knew the James family, the mill had not been good to them. They had enjoyed the mountain freshness, the smells of pine and sawdust, and had lived frugally from the sale of rough lumber. Clyde was a man, I a boy. His father had but one arm; he had accidentally sawed off the other. The saw had literally bitten off the arm that fed it. Clyde too became a victim of the mill—he surrendered a leg to the teeth of the saw. Then, handicapped, the James family gave up the mill.

At the time the sawmill closed, Clyde lived with his wife and child in a cabin of his own deep in the woods not far from the mill. He knew the mountain men, the hunters, the range riders, the cowboys, and some of the troublemakers who fled from the law by crossing into Wyoming not far from his home. Out of work, he seized the opportunity to go into business to fill the needs of some of his liberal friends who had grown thirsty through Prohibition.

At this time Mose Koyle had changed the sign above the door of his establishment in Victor from "Saloon" to "Pool Hall." I don't know if he ever dealt in Clyde James's brew, but I do know that the Kay and Murphy men and others at Saturday night dances entertained us younger, sober boys with loosened tongues, talking about the potency of Clyde's "still swill," and how after imbibing and becoming bold with drink, they tormented each other into fistfights on the green in front of the dance hall.

Ardent prohibitionists and church leaders of the valley, knowing of their inability to get federal officers to deal with their liquor problem, stirred the sheriff into action against the operation of the still. In response the sheriff went to Clyde's home (the still was hidden some distance away) and told him he knew of his illegal business and ordered him to abandon it. Clyde ignored the orders and the church became more demanding and the sheriff more adamant.

When the meadowlarks sang their spring song that year, Clyde's wife's young, unmarried sister came to spend summer vacation with them in the freedom and freshness of mountain air. Then as months passed the sister stayed until snow time, when callers noted that the girl's girth had suddenly broadened. Scandalous news—voiced in town, in pool hall, barber shop, post office, and backyards—began, "Have you heard . . . Clyde James . . . his sister-in-law . . . pregnant?"

At this time Clyde had adjusted to the loss of a leg and showed but little handicap in mobility. Well-proportioned physically, with dark hair and eyes, olive skin, a cleanshaven face, his appearance never offended, nor did his mellifluous voice so incongruent with his monosyllabic vocabulary.

The bishop said, "Clyde, you are breaking the laws of man and of God."

Clyde answered softly, "I mind my own business—don't know about God—I don't push nothin' on nobody, just give 'em what they ask for. It's a free country."

Clyde ignored the gossip and joined the pool-hall gang as freely and confidently as ever. Evening's chill again led Mose Koyle to build a fire in the potbellied stove, and men in his place of business sat in chairs around it chatting and spitting in the ash tray, pulled out now to serve as a spittoon.

The proprietor said to Clyde, "I'm worried about you."

"Why the hell?" said Clyde.

"The sheriff's goin' ta lock you up!" said Mose.

"He ain't got nothin' on me," Clyde answered. "Nobody can get me because nobody has seen me sell nothin' to nobody. My business is in Wyoming an' when he comes to my house, I go acrost the line an' laugh at him while he smells old 'corny.' "

The listeners laughed.

Someone said, "Clyde, I heard that you bedded down in the pine grass up there with your wife's sister."

"Sure! Hell, yes!" said Clyde. "It's like this, if anyone lays money or anything else that I like on the table, to get something I got to give 'em ta make 'em happy, whether it's a shot of 'corn' or anything else, I never turn 'em down."

HARVEY ROBERTSON, THE PRISONER

College and profession lured me away from my homeland for seven years. Then I returned in 1930 to be superintendent of schools for the small twelve-teacher system. During the four years I held that position, Harvey Robertson, a unique character, climbed through high school. He died a prison inmate in Colorado State Prison in Canon City, Colorado, in 1965.

When in high school, though an orphan living alone, he kept himself neat and clean and attended school regularly; he loved literature, art, drama, music, and dance. Unlike his brothers and sister, he spoke impeccable English. But he was effeminate, giggly, and somewhat fickle. He became "queered" by his peers and was given the nickname "Pansy." He had had no religious training, no Christian upbringing. Now a social outcast, he saw values in the dominant church in the valley and joined. He had no problem with the church, for his outward behavior was in keeping with church standards. Then he fell in love with Golda Sherman, a quiet, serious girl of sound integrity. These two, after graduation from high school, were married.

Harvey could hardly be called a good member of society or a good family man; he was too unstable, too irresponsible. As children came to his home, he allowed his weaknesses to prosper and his strengths to be neglected.

A general grocery clerk, he provided a meager livelihood for a growing family, along with periodic subsidies from income his wife earned from work outside the home. Harvey never complained, never scolded, never used bad language, never cursed or struck his children or wife, never looked or acted like a bum, and, unfortunately, never ever revered truth. He could tell lies with complete abandon. In fact, a great challenge to family tranquility came through his words falling into imbalance with truth. He giggled his way into and out of open falsehood.

"You bought a new pair of shoes," said Golda, "with your own closet full of shoes and the children barefoot."

"They were gifts," he said.

Later a canceled check came from the bank made out to the shoe store.

"You did not come home after work last night until after midnight," said Golda.

"I had to clean up the store after it closed," explained Harvey.

"You took dress clothes and shoes with you to work. I know you went dancing," Golda argued.

Harvey laughed.

Out of this disregard for truth came marital dissension that ballooned into the divorce courts. Then, without the support of his wife and family, he failed utterly. He got into trouble with the law, not for crimes of violence, but for crimes of passion, for he loved people and had no capacity to hate—his were crimes of emotional gratification. In 1959, at the age of forty-six, he was convicted and incarcerated in prison. Six years later, while still in prison, he died of cancer.

A daughter, Nyla Brookshire, visited Harvey in prison and, in his final years of struggle with disease, gave him support and love. She showed me many papers after Harvey's death, copies of a prison paper, a publication which I discovered Harvey had sponsored and edited. With these papers were others, most notable of which were testimonials written of him, and letters to him, written by fellow prisoners, Colorado state felons, who had become his friends. I read them. I found that these men—murderers, rapists, thieves, all at odds with the law—had written notes full of deep sentiment. Some were well written, some almost illiterate. One read, "Harvey learnt me many good things no mother never learnt me what she should."

From these papers I learned that Harvey had not only edited the prison paper, he had written for it, had organized and directed a singing group, had taught literature classes, had taught the prisoners things of beauty and truth.

At his funeral a speaker said, "Here was a man of worth who has been called to meet death, a man who could not manage his own life well, who had to be restricted and confined and who, there in prison, found a freedom and release."

The Matriarch, 1910–1952

RETURN TO THE VALLEY

The years of my mother's widowhood from the death of Peter Durney and her marriage to William Avery were the years of my youth, when time ran slowly and sensitivity waxed strong. Those were the years when Mother played the role of family mentor, teacher by example and precept of industry, frugality, integrity, and love of truth and beauty.

I thought we were poor; yet we never found the cupboard bare, never dressed in rags, never passed a winter without shoes and overshoes, warm clothes, and shelter, never seriously froze a foot or a toe. We lived as healthfully and happily as most homemakers of the day.

Mother believed in the philosophy of the folk song:

Waste not, want not is the practice that I teach,
Let your watchword be dispatch and practice what you preach,
Do not let your chances like sunbeams pass you by,
For you'll never miss the water till the well runs dry.

No visions fill my memory of sitting on Mother's lap. She always used her hands when sitting—sewing, knitting, darning, patching, mending.

One year, before adolescence lengthened my legs, Mother bought overalls for me to fit my waist, but in length the longest available, some eight inches longer than my legs, the price being the same; then she cut off the excess length and made denim mittens for me.

When the wool stockings she knit for me wore out in the feet, she allowed me to unravel the good parts, wind the yarn into a ball, and sew a binding on the outside to keep it from unwinding. Yarn balls of this type, though less resilient than rubber balls or baseballs, were not bad, and mine was prettier than other children's because Mother taught her children to wind them tight and bind them beautifully in even stitching with red carpet warp.

Our home at the edge of town joined the eighty-acre farm, twenty acres of which was in cultivation. There we lived, kept four or five cows, one horse, a flock of chickens, and two pigs. These chickens and pigs processed every calorie of garbage we had into eggs and meat. My three older sisters assisted their mother, the forceful foreman of the farm, in gardening, growing vegetables and berries, and caring for animals. I learned to work; at eight I learned to squeeze milk from contented cows.

Uncle Stephen rented and ran our other place, the Durney farm, which produced little more profit than enough to pay all the taxes and interest on the mortgage.

Seeing Mother's struggle for survival, Uncle consulted the county commissioners, soliciting for her a widow's pension. In response Ben Jones came to our home one day to determine the need.

"Mrs. Durney," he said as he sat in our comfortable living room, "your home is nice, better equipped than most homes in the county."

"Yes," answered Mother, "this is my home and furniture, household things I had before I became a widow. It is not food and clothes for my family and fuel to keep us warm."

She did not get the pension.

To supplement the meager farm income, Mother went into the carpet-weaving business. She ordered the loom of latest automatic make, assembled it, ordered warp of various colors, and accepted carpet rags stripped and sewed together for custom weaving. For a number of years we were never out of work. The warp and woof of our lives were tied up with carpet rags. We all worked industriously on the family project. Mother planned beautiful designs for rugs and carpets, managed all orders, supervised, and labored. The little children, Gordon and Stenna, filled shuttles with carpet rags, and the older ones helped in threading the loom and weaving.

Mother sold her services cheaply, always making sure to give full value for her work. She charged twelve and a half cents a yard for weaving. At that price the family did well to earn twenty-five dollars a month.

After William Avery married Mother and had operated her farms for a few years, he received a lucrative offer from Austin Brothers Sheep Company to return to management of the company. This he accepted, necessitating a move to Snake River Valley. There he and Mother prospered and established a lovely home. A decade later he became a victim of cardiac insufficiency and died, leaving Mother a widow for the third time. Then she lived alone.

In those quiet years came a time when she and I experienced a nostalgic visit to our homeland. As we entered the valley from Pine Creek Pass, tears welled up in her eyes. "This is my homeland," she said. "I never really felt at home away from the mountains."

"You are a Naomi," I said, "returning to Israel from Moab."

"Life was good here," she said.

"Good?" I said. "Cold, cold winters—ice freezing in the teakettle on the kitchen stove—snowdrifts so high around the house that we couldn't see out!"

"Snow is clean and beautiful," she explained. "Pines are in their best dress when flocked with snow."

"But," I said, "you must admit you have it better now, a milder climate, a convenient, modern home, an easier life."

"Ease is not a virtue to seek for young, vigorous people," she said. "The pursuit of easy things makes people weak."

She paused and for a moment we sat in silence. Then she spoke again: "Pleasure comes through striving and surviving."

"This valley is static," I said. "There are no more people here than there were thirty years ago. The place has regressed; it is not the same. The impressive stone two-story schoolhouse is gone—burned down; the railroad is gone; the depot is now a warehouse; the Killpack Hotel is gone; the bank long since was closed and the building lies empty . . ."

"I love the town," Mother interrupted. "It is a jewel in the mountains."

This was becoming a debate, I realized, and I was arguing the negative side. Was I a lover of argument? No, I told myself in rationalization, just analytic.

"Our old home has survived," Mother said. "The shade trees you and I planted, now too big to reach around, are old like me, but the mountains, the flowers, the clover, the fresh air, sunshine, clouds, and sky are the same."

We visited the cemetery, she and I, experiencing more deeply the resting zones of past experience.

"I want to be buried here by your father," she said.

"You do?" I exclaimed. "You buried Dad Avery in Grove City Cemetery and you have a lot there by him, and a joint gravestone bearing his name and yours."

"It was a mistake," she said, "a temporary sorrow—he should have been buried by his first wife, the mother of his children. I must be by my first husband, the father of four of my children. This is the place where I belong."

"Do you remember," I asked as we stood by my father's grave, "how long ago graves were covered with a mound of earth and how we came here one spring and found Father's grave concave instead of convex?"

"His coffin had rotted," she said. "You and I rounded the grave up again with earth."

We remembered that day, the pole fence enclosing the cemetery with weathered poles and cross posts, and the sagebrush and sunflowers on unused portions of the burial ground. Now the leveled graves with lawn covering, the neat wire fence around, the even roadways—all these showed respect for the dead memorialized there.

"This is a peaceful spot," Mother said, as if telling herself.

We left the Basin, passed again over Pine Creek Pass. Mother returned to her home and I drove on to mine, and the daily routine of life went on.

In 1952, after Mother's death, I returned alone to the cemetery. There I meditated, listened to the voices of the spirit. A resurrection of these dead burst into my soul—a chorus of voices ranging from the soft alto of Grandma Rice to the bass boom of Whispering Ed, the southern drawl of Pleasant Sherman to the foreign accent of George Rust—on and on, voices and more voices. The solo part in the chorus among Grandma Cheney, Father, Stepfather Durney, Aunt Mary, Cousin Marion, and all the rest came from Mother—a message of love.

Aroused from reverie, I became aware of the view of the housetops in the town a mile or so away. There stood the old home, its roof peeking through the elm trees. Beyond it rose the impressive tower of the sandstone church. In the soft breeze I caught the sweet scent of pine trees and sagebrush. I saw the ridge above the Durney farm and the stretch of the Teton Mountains.

No man here, I knew, was a man without a country; no woman here was without roots in the good earth. How strong they were! How strong was their valley!